A Guide to Military History on the Internet

D1327732

A Guide to Military History on the Internet

Simon Fowler

Pen & Sword
FAMILY HISTORY

WANDSWORTH LIBRARY SERVICE

First published in Great Britain in 2007 by
PEN & SWORD FAMILY HISTORY
an imprint of
Pen & Sword Books Ltd
47 Church Street
Barnsley
South Yorkshire
S70 2AS

Copyright © Simon Fowler 2007

ISBN 978 1 84415 606 1

The right of Simon Fowler to be identified as Author of this Work has been
asserted by him in accordance with the Copyright,
Designs and Patents Act 1988.

A CIP catalogue record for this book is
available from the British Library.

*All rights reserved. No part of this book may be reproduced or transmitted in any form or
by any means, electronic or mechanical including photocopying, recording or by any
information storage and retrieval system, without permission from the Publisher in
writing.*

Typeset in Palatino and Optima by
Phoenix Typesetting, Auldgirth, Dumfriesshire

LONDON BOROUGH OF WANDSWORTH	
501177213	
Askews	08-Nov-2007
025.06355009 FOWL	£9.99
	WWX0002500/0060

Pen & Sword Aviation, Pen & Sword Maritime, Pen & Sword Military, Wharncliffe
Local History, Pen & Sword Select, Pen & Sword Military Classics and Leo
Cooper.

For a complete list of Pen & Sword titles please contact
PEN & SWORD BOOKS LIMITED
47 Church Street, Barnsley, South Yorkshire, S70 2AS, England
E-mail: enquiries@pen-and-sword.co.uk
Website: www.pen-and-sword.co.uk

CONTENTS

ACKNOWLEDGEMENTS

I'm grateful to Rupert Harding for his patience in waiting for this manuscript and making some suggestions about form and content. Sylvia Levi helped proof-read the text and Mike Booker suggested some useful websites. Chris Summerville knocked an unwieldy manuscript into shape in double-quick time.

INTRODUCTION

It seems absurd – the easier it is to do research online, the more books listing websites seem to be published. And they are all very popular. If you've picked up this book in a shop and are wondering why you should buy it, here are two reasons (apart from keeping the author and publisher in the styles to which they would like to become accustomed!):

1. There are thousands of websites devoted to British military history: Google comes up with 1,150,000 sites with pages on RAF history alone. Do you really want to go through all of them to find the one you want? I have saved you the trouble of trawling through Google and the other search engines. All you need do is type the website address (URL) into your browser.

2. Experienced researchers will tell you that there is an awful lot of rubbish out there in cyberworld, and a depressing amount of it relates to military history. I have selected what I think are the best sites: that is, those websites that contain accurate information, do not unnecessarily duplicate material from other sites, and which look reasonably attractive and literate. This last point is often the prime indicator that the site is worth a visit.

The scope of this volume is roughly between the Norman Invasion in 1066 and the Good Friday Agreement in 1998, which saw the beginning of the end of British military activity in North Ireland. The book largely contains sites relating to Britain and British military history. That is, they are about:

- The three services and their history.

- Individual units, such as ships, regiments and RAF squadrons (but few websites created by old comrade associations are included unless they contain material likely to be of interest to non-members).

- Servicemen and women (either individuals or groups, such as an aircrew or platoon) where the information provided is of wider interest than just to the immediate family or descendents.

- Wars (such as to the two world wars), individual campaigns and associated battles (e.g. Zulu Wars or Rorke's Drift).

- Tangential subjects, such as the merchant marine, which has always close links to the Royal Navy.

- Sources and guidance to researching military history.

- Relevant mailing lists and related resources.

I have also included websites about Commonwealth forces (particularly the Australians and Canadians) plus a selection of sites relating to other nations' experiences of the two world wars (American, French, German etc.). I have also included websites featuring other periods that seemed particularly interesting.

Readers, however, should note there are no websites here about:

- The armed forces today or the immediate past, unless there is some interesting historical content or perhaps offer an interesting overview of the services in the early 21st century.

- The loonier end of military history. If you want to know why Churchill was a secret Nazi agent, then this is not the book for you. Nor do I describe UFOs and any alleged cover-ups relating to them. On the other hand, see p. 209 for a list of ten of the most unusual or fun sites I came across during the course of my researches.

Accuracy

So far as possible the addresses are all accurate at the time of writing: that is April–May 2007. Inevitably a few will have changed by the time you read this or, occasionally, a site may have disappeared altogether. Apparently, the average life of a website is 44 days and certainly, when I was researching this book, I reckon that well over a quarter of sites I tried to visit no longer existed, and a few even disappeared while the book was being written. If you can't find a site, here are a couple of handy tips:

- Type the subject into Google (or another search engine) and see what comes up.

- See whether there is a link to it from a related website.

- Old pages from many sites are stored by the Internet Archive (also known as the Way Back When Machine) at www.archive.org, so if a site is no longer functioning you should be able to get some idea of what it contained.

Inevitably I will have missed a few sites. If I have left out your personal site or a favourite website that you find particularly useful – provided it meets the criteria listed above – why not nominate it? Contact me via the publishers and I'll try to include it in the second edition.

Using Search Engines Effectively

If there is no reference to a particular unit or piece of kit in this book, you might want to search for it direct. The way to do this is by using a search engine that will trawl the internet and come up with hundreds, possibly thousands, of choices. By far the most popular is Google (www.google.co.uk), but there are others, which may be worth checking out. The chances are that they will turn up slightly different results:

- www.altavista.com

- http://uk.ask.com

- http://uk.msn.com

- http://uk.yahoo.com

In addition, www.dogpile.com and www.hotbot.com search a number of different search engines and come up with what they regard as the most relevant sites.

You can narrow your searches by using what are known as Boolean operators or commands. They are not as complicated as they first seem – a simple guide can be found at www.internettutorials.net/boolean.html.

Putting the subject you are looking for in speech marks may help too. Type in 'HMS' and 'Victory' will come up with all sites that include the words 'HMS' and 'Victory'. 'HMS Victory' will only find sites with the phrase 'HMS Victory'. In most cases this is enough to find the information you want, but if you want to find references to Nelson and HMS *Victory* you can type in 'HMS Victory' AND 'Nelson' or 'HMS Victory+Nelson', or, to refine the search further, 'HMS Victory' AND 'Horatio Nelson' (in many cases you can omit AND or +). If you want to read about HMS *Victory* without reference to Nelson, you can type 'HMS Victory' NOT Nelson or 'HMS Victory-Nelson'. Occasionally you want to find sites relating to different subjects, so use the command OR (for example 'HMS Victory' OR 'Nelson'). It is important to put the Boolean command in capital letters (AND, OR, NOT).

There are other commands, and the Boolean logic employed works slightly

differently depending on the search engine you are using. A full introduction can be found at http://searchenginewatch.com/showPage.html?page=2155991.

Technical Requirements

The fact that you have bought this book suggests you have access to the internet at home or possibly at work. If you haven't already upgraded it is well worth considering broadband, which means that sites load much quicker and you can easily play video and sound clips. This will cost about £20 a month, although it is possible to get better deals. Your internet service provider (ISP) or telephone company will be able to advise (or visit www.broadband.co.uk for comparisons between the various services). I use a cable service, Virgin Media, which I have found very good and problem free.

It is also well worth acquiring the free Adobe Acrobat Reader plug-in, which allows you to read PDF files – usually printed booklets or brochures that have been encapsulated in this format to make them quick to download – from www.adobe.com/products/acrobat/readstep2.html. The product is easy to download and is idiot proof. However, avoid buying any of the Adobe Acrobat products, unless you want to create PDFs of your own.

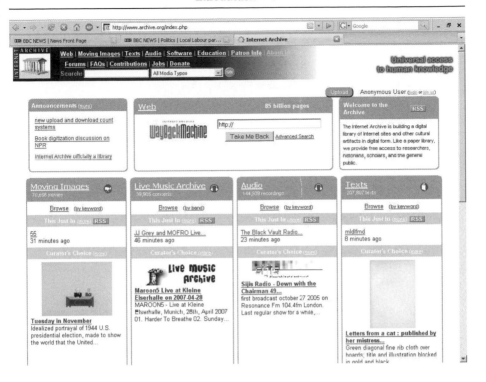

Less useful is the Flash plug-in, which allows you to view moving images. In the early days of the internet, many sites provided such pages, generally as an introduction to the site, which proved unpopular with users as they were an expensive addition to the telephone bill. Fortunately, where you come across such a page and don't want to waste your time and money you can normally skip it.

The web browser provided on most computers is Microsoft's Internet Explorer: version 7 was launched at the end of 2006. Somewhat better is Mozilla Firefox, which can be downloaded for free from www.mozilla.org. All the sites in this book were checked using Firefox – occasionally websites don't like this browser, in which case you might need to switch back to Internet Explorer. Mozilla also offers an email program called Thunderbird, which has the advantage of receiving far fewer viruses and other nasties than Microsoft Outlook Express.

Chapter 1

GENERAL RESOURCES

Websites

If you are unsure of your military history (e.g. when battles were fought or when the RAF was formed) there are a number of websites that will provide at least some background. To my mind, the best is Wikipedia (http://en.wikipedia.org), which is an on-line encyclopaedia compiled by its users. Anybody can add or amend almost all of the entries, which may seem a little odd, but the results are largely accurate and generally free of bias. If you spot anything that is wrong you can always change it. Most of the main topics in British military history are covered, and many of the more obscure ones as well.

Take the entry for HMS *Victory*, for example: there is a history of Nelson's flagship, the admirals who have hoisted their flag on her, the dimensions of the ship, photographs and links to related entries, from shipworm to Admiral Sir James Burnell-Nugent, as well as a number of external websites. At the top of the entry you can read (and contribute) to the discussion on what needs to be changed or improved in the entry.

If you want to write or review entries seriously, then it is worth joining the rather grandly named British Military History Taskforce. More details at http://en.wikipedia.org/wiki/Wikipedia:WikiProject_Military_history/British_military_history_task_force.

There are several other on-line encyclopaedias, but in general the entries are rather short and often not very satisfactory. They include:

- http://encarta.msn.com

- www.britannica.com

In addition, there are a number of sites that provide articles and other resources for the military historian, particular those interested in battles or campaigns:

The World History Database at www.badley.info/history provides lots of very basic information, so it is easy to check the dates of particular battles or military commanders.

It can be hard to find casualty figures for wars and campaigns, but http://users.erols.com/mwhite28/warstat0.htm#EnglCW offers 'an incomplete listing of some very bad things that happened before the twentieth century', including the Hundred Years War (c 185,000 men died) and the English Civil War (c 84,300). It also provides a list of the 20 most violent events in human history, beginning with the Second World War, which saw the deaths of 55 million.

http://militaryhistory.suite101.com – short essays on various aspects of military history. It is especially good for the Crimean War.

www.christopherlong.co.uk – pieces by a British journalist (and sheep breeder) mainly on the two world wars.

www.eyewitnesstohistory.com – selected eyewitness accounts of great events with an American emphasis.

www.hillsdale.edu/personal/stewart/war – a personal website maintained by a history professor at a college in Michigan, containing many documents, diary extracts, despatches and letters used in his teaching.

www.historyofwar.org/main.html – very good Anglo-American introduction with short descriptions of wars, battles, biographies of military commanders and military concepts.

www.spartacus.schoolnet.co.uk – although designed for schools it contains many short informative essays on military themes and heroes. A similar site, again intended for students, is www.historylearningsite.co.uk.

www.stephen-stratford.co.uk/index.htm – a series of essays on the military history of the twentieth century, mainly, of course, for the two world wars, with information about medals, spying, war crimes and courts martial. There are also pages on crime history and infamous murders.

www.wtj.com – mainly American, but there are articles and extracts from records relating to the two world wars and Napoleonic wars.

www.geocities.com/davidbofinger/ah.htm – pages of alternative histories, particularly interesting for the Second World War.

www.balagan.org.uk/war/index.htm – combines military modelling, wargaming and military history, particularly the Carlist Wars in Spain in the nineteenth century, the Arab-Israeli wars since 1948 and New Zealanders in Italy during the Second World War.

www.greatnorthernpublishing.co.uk publishes magazines about the two world wars as well as, ahem, a tasteful magazine of pornographic literature.

Overseas Websites

There are a number of excellent websites relating to the military history of Commonwealth countries:

All researchers of Australian military history, or individuals who served with the Australian forces, should visit www.awm.gov.au – the superb site of the Australian War Memorial in Canberra. It has huge resources for all the wars in which Australia took part, from the Boer War to the present day. It is one of my top ten websites (see p. 203).

www.diggerhistory.info is dedicated to the unofficial history of Australian and New Zealand armed forces during the twentieth century. Despite an unpromising homepage it is a treasure trove of information, some of which is taken from publications of the period. There's also material about American, Canadian and British armed forces.

Another superb site is at www.cmhg.gc.ca. The excellent Canadian Military History Gateway has links to thousands of articles and clips from radio and TV programmes. It's easy to use and very informative.

http://regimentalrogue.tripod.com/index.htm is an unusual site with many pages on the history of the Canadian and British armies, particularly looking at the officer classes from the Boer War until the 1960s.

The Canadian War Museum in Ottawa at www.warmuseum.ca/cwm/cwme.asp has some interesting pages and a number of on-line exhibitions.

http://web.mala.bc.ca/davies/Letters.Images/homepage.htm has collections of letters sent by Canadian soldiers over the past hundred years or so.

www.military.ie/military_archives has details of the Irish Military Archives in Dublin, which has papers of the Irish Army and other services since Partition in 1921.

Many records for New Zealanders are held by Archives New Zealand in Wellington. Their holdings of military material are described in a leaflet that can be downloaded in a PDF file from www.archives.govt.nz/docs/pdfs/ Ref_Guide_War.pdf.

Books

Finding information on websites is all very well and good, but there may come a time when you want to do your own research. Most people are happy enough to look up their family tree or a particular serviceman, but there is nothing to stop you from studying a particular campaign, ship or aircraft in more detail.

A good first step is to read up on the subject. The British Library Public Catalogue (http://blpc.bl.uk) will supply you with details of virtually every book ever published in Britain. And your local library can order most books through the inter-library loan service for a few pence.

You can find out what is currently in print by visiting the Amazon website (www.amazon.co.uk): most bookshops can order any book currently in print for you – this is often cheaper and quicker than ordering via Amazon. Many publishers also give discounts if you order direct from them. For example, Pen & Sword (www.pen-and-sword.co.uk), the excellent publishers of this volume, offer 20 per cent on new titles plus free postage and packing on all orders.

Not everything is still in print of course. But even the most obscure second-hand books can be found via www.abebooks.co.uk. An alternative is to check whether a particular book is being sold on eBay (www.ebay.co.uk).

There are also a number of booksellers who specialise in new or second-hand military history. One of the largest, with a first-rate on-line catalogue, is the Naval & Military Press (www.naval-military-press.com). There are several specialist booksellers devoted to the Second World War: http://worldwartwobooks.com is based in rural Wales (although the stock seems to be very much for the enthusiast), while Stone and Stone, an American specialist bookseller, has many thousands of pages related to books about the war at www.sonic.net/~bstone.

Archives, Libraries And Museums

Eventually you may want to use original archive material, which may prove to be time-consuming but in return is deeply addictive and rewarding. Some material, mainly of interest to family historians, has been digitised and images made online for a fee. This is described in the next chapter.

Otherwise you will have to visit an archive to look through the records for yourself. These documents can be found in one of several places: a national repository or museum, a regimental or service museum, or less often a local studies library or county record office.

Most records of the armed forces are held at the National Archives (formerly the Public Record Office) (www.nationalarchives.gov.uk), or at national museums dedicated to the services such as the National Army Museum (www.national-army-museum.ac.uk), the Royal Naval Museum (www.royalnavalmuseum.org) and the RAF Museum (www.rafmuseum.org.uk) and, for the twentieth century, the Imperial War Museum (www.iwm.org.uk). These institutions' websites all have pages about their archival and library holdings and offer advice about undertaking research there.

There are also national archives in Scotland (www.nas.gov.uk), Northern Ireland (www.proni.gov.uk) and the Republic of Ireland (www.nationalarchives.ie), although none of these have particularly large collections of material relating to the British armed forces. However, the National War Museum of Scotland in Edinburgh Castle has considerable holdings for Scottish regiments (www.nms.ac.uk/warmuseumhomepage.aspx).

Every English, and almost all Welsh, counties have a local record office and most towns have a local studies or history centre and they all have websites of varying degrees of usefulness. They may, for example, have material relating to local militia regiments or Home Guard units For example, Gloucestershire Archives has a list of military records in WORD format at www.gloucestershire.gov.uk/media/word/r/0/Military%20handlist%20working%20version%20for%20web%20RS.doc.

The ARCHON section of The National Archives website (www.nationalarchives.gov.uk/archon) provides links to local record offices. It can be much harder however to track down local studies libraries, particularly ones outside your area. You can however find most addresses at www.familia.org.uk.

A few archives and museums have on-line catalogues to their holdings, so you can check exactly what have they and note down call or item numbers which can help your research if you did decide to visit. The National Archives (TNA) even allows you to order three documents in advance of your visit. TNA's catalogue is at www.nationalarchives.gov.uk/catalogue and the IWM catalogue at www.iwmcollections.org.uk.

Access to Archives (www.a2a.org.uk) is in effect a nationwide catalogue to the holdings of local archives in England – some 400 at the last count – it is not complete and military history is not its main focus, although it does include material from the National

Army Museum and British Library Oriental and India Office Collections (which has lots about the Indian Army). Similar sites are:

- www.archivesnetworkwales.info – for Wales

- www.archiveshub.ac.uk – for university libraries and archives

- www.nationalarchives.gov.uk/nra – where private papers and records of businesses and organisations are to be found

- www.scan.org.uk – for Scotland

There are also networks of smaller official or semi-official service museums, most of which maintain an archive or library (see Chapter 4). If, for example, you are researching a particular regiment, ship or squadron you may need to contact them as well as the national repositories.

Chief among them is the Imperial War Museum in London, where behind the scenes there are numerous collections of documents, printed books, art, exhibits and firearms, photographs and film and sound archive, which is either on display or available to serious researchers free. The Collection has a wealth of material, including:

- 19,000 painting, drawings and sculptures

- 15,000 posters

- 120 million feet of cine film

- 10,000 hours of videotape

- 36,000 hours of historical sound recordings

- 6 million photographs, negatives and transparencies

- 270,000 items in the library

Many items are described on the on-line catalogue at http://collections.iwm.org.uk. I have to say I find the catalogue both confusing and very limited in its scope.

Regimental museums may have archival material relating to their regiment or corps, although their holdings vary greatly. Certainly they should have collections of photographs, the regimental journal and may be able to tell you more about the men (particularly officers) who served in the regiment. Links to regimental and corps museums (and both sites offer advice on research in general) can be found at www.armymuseums.org.uk and www.army.mod.uk/museums.

The best place to start researching naval and maritime history is the PORT Maritime Information Gateway maintained by the National Maritime Museum at www.port.nmm.ac.uk. Subject gateways provide access to searchable and browseable catalogues of Internet based resources, all of which have been quality controlled or assessed before inclusion. Everything is grouped into twenty subject-headings, such as 'conflicts at sea' or 'careers' and further subdivided into smaller topics.

There are over a hundred aviation museums in the UK (for details see Chapter 4). The most important is the RAF Museum, which has a comprehensive archive and library. Some of the artefact collection can now be searched using the Navigator catalogue. www.rafmuseum.org.uk

Films

The campaigns of the twentieth century, and life in the services, have been recorded on film. The best place to start is www.britishpathe.com, where it is possible to download newsreel clips made by British Pathé between the Boer War and the late 1960s. It is a superb resource and it is free and easy to use. The quality of downloads is sometimes poor, although if you want better quality footage you can pay for it. Some material, for example scenes of shell-shocked men at Netley Hospital, is still very disturbing even after ninety years.

The largest collection of strictly military films and related material is held by the Imperial War Museum. The collection is described at http://collections.iwm.org.uk/server/show/nav.00g004. It is not possible to download any material, although many of the more interesting films have been released on commercial video or DVDs. However, there is an on-line catalogue at www.iwmcollections.org.uk/qryFilm.asp, which may help if you are looking for footage of a particular event or incident.

Occasionally, you may find short clips on websites. Where this is the case this is noted in the description

Maps

From the sixteenth century maps have been an essential element of warfare, used for planning campaigns and battles, and for assessing the results thereafter. The National Archives, British Library, Imperial War Museum and National Army and Maritime museums all have large collections.

There are a fair number of sites containing facsimiles of maps or information about original maps and map libraries. One place to start is by visiting http://users.erols.com/mwhite28/maplinks.htm, with lots of links to websites containing maps, including those for wars from the medieval period. You may need to scroll down to find what you want. Also useful is http://oddens.geog.uu.nl/index.php, which claims to have 21,000 links to map-related websites.

Paintings And Photographs

Battlefields, ships and aircraft have long been a favourite subject for painters, in part because there is always a demand for their work. There are surprisingly few sites devoted to the subject. Chief among them is Maritime Art Greenwich at the National Maritime Museum (www.nmm.ac.uk/mag), which is a resource combining subject expertise and the National Maritime Museum's oil painting collection. The website offers a searchable database of selected paintings plus in-depth content on some of the major themes of maritime art.

You can see (and of course buy) modern military aviation and maritime paintings and reproductions from a number of sites, including www.regimental-art.com/index.html, www.avart.co.uk and www.oliversart.com. Although technically perfect it always seems to me that such paintings lack life, but then the machines are the stars and any humans are merely the support act.

Artefacts And Collectables

There are a number of sites where you can buy and sell militaria, such as badges or medals. Perhaps the biggest is eBay (www.ebay.co.uk), which is extremely easy to use. The problem with eBay (and no doubt with other sites) is that many items on sale are either reproductions or fake. This should be made clear in the seller's description, but if an item is being sold suspiciously cheaply then you are right to be suspicious.

A list of dealers in militaria worldwide can be found at www.google.com/Top/Shopping/Antiques_and_Collectibles/Militaria. But be prepared to plough through all the American and German sites to find what you want.

Professional Researchers

There may come a time in your research when you might want to employ a professional researcher (sometimes called independent researchers or record agents) to help. Many are very good, a few appalling. Some maintain websites, which can give a fair idea of how capable and knowledgeable a person is.

The National Archives maintains a list of independent researchers at www.nationalarchives.gov.uk/irlist. Before contacting anybody on their list you should read the advice on the home page.

In addition, museums or local record offices may be able to suggest more specialist researchers.

Creating Your Own Website

Once you have completed your own research you might want to think about creating your own website, in order to share your research with others of like mind. As you will see, hundreds of researchers and enthusiasts have taken up the challenge. Although it is fairly easy to do, the fashion for creating websites seems to have largely passed, possibly because they must be maintained (and ideally updated) on a regular basis. An example of what not to do is my own site, www.sfowler.force9.co.uk, which has lain neglected since 2001.

Most Internet Service Providers (ISPs) will offer a certain amount of free (and sometimes limited) webspace for you to create your own website. Alternatively, you can approach a company to host your site. This might cost up to £100 a year, but it does mean you can use your own internet address (such as www.penwin.co.uk), plus there will be much space available, and they may help you design and layout your site. Four such companies are:

- www.doyourownsite.co.uk

- www.fasthosts.co.uk

- www.moonfruit.co.uk

- www.strato-hosting.co.uk

However, there are many others that may be more suitable for your needs. An alternative is Mr Site, at www.mrsite.co.uk, whose software will build a website for you. It is firmly aimed at small businesses and from my experience (see www.penwin.co.uk) is rather limited. There are a few other sites that will help you build your own website, such as

- www.howtocreate.co.uk

- www.2createawebsite.com

- www.1stsitefree.com

- www.fasthosts.co.uk/hosting/sitebuilder

Except for the simplest sites, you will need web builder or editing software. A hosting company or ISP may supply the software, or you may have it installed on your computer, such as Microsoft Publisher. Occasionally computer magazines may include programmes on their front cover discs: this may be an old version, but should be enough to get you started. But before you begin, it is important to know what you want to put up. You should consider the following:

- What do I want the site to achieve?

- Who is the site aimed at?

- What content is the site going to contain?

- How often do I want to update the site?

Once you have the answers to these questions you can start planning your site. The more thought and attention to detail invested during the planning stage, the easier it will be to create and maintain your website.

Design and layout is important. At the very least, each page should contain a link back to the home page. You should not have to scroll down too far to find what you want. The design should be uncluttered and clear. Personally, I would avoid bright colours, which are off-putting and wearying on the eye. And avoid advertisements (again very irritating for the visitor), particularly pop-ups, although of course they may generate a little income. A design I particularly like is www.king-emperor.com.

Recent Technology

An increasingly popular alternative is the blog or weblog, basically maintaining an on-line diary of your thoughts and activities. They are easy to set up and require little maintenance, but think about whom might be interested in what you have to say. Most blogs are little visited, usually with good reason. Some interesting examples of military history blogs can be found at

- http://milhist.blogspot.com

- http://warhistorian.org/wordpress/index.php

- http://airminded.org

- http://chailey1418.blogspot.com

Others are mentioned in the appropriate place below. If you are tempted to set up your own, visit www.blogger.com/start.

It is also possible to upload videos and photographs to a variety of sites. The best-known one for video clips is YouTube at www.youtube.com. For example, www.youtube.com/watch?v=uitTP8sNNuo&mode=related&search= has a four-minute home movie of life on-board HMS *Plymouth* in 1972, consisting largely of barely clad young men posing for the camera. For photographs, look at Flickr www.flickr.com. Both are indexed after a fashion, but even so, expect to trawl through lots of irrelevant sites posted by American teenagers.

A more specialist alternative is www.militaryimages.net, which contains a number of different forums where members can post photographs, posters and military art. Inevitably it is a bit hit-and-miss, but there are some good things here.

There are increasing numbers of aerial and satellite photographs available through software, such as Google Earth (http://earth.google.com), which may include war memorials and battlefield sites, as well as contemporary military installations. For example, www.satellite-sightseer.com/id/3678/Italy//Cassino/Battle_of_Monte_ Cassino__Polish_Cemetery offers a view of the Polish cemetery at Monte Cassino in Italy, where 1,150 brave soldiers have their last resting-place.

Chapter 2

RESEARCHING INDIVIDUALS

Although family history has been transformed by the internet, people researching military ancestors, or other individuals who served in the armed forces, have so far not been particularly well served. However, this will change over the next few years as Ancestry, FindMyPast and other companies increasingly put digitised images of military records online. Even so, there is already a vast amount of material on the web – most of the websites described in this book, for example, can be used to provide some background information about an individual's military service.

However, before you start, you need to be certain which service an ancestor was with (Army, Royal Navy, including Royal Marines and Fleet Air Arm, and from April 1918 the Royal Air Force) and roughly when they served. It is also useful to know which Army unit (Royal Artillery, Royal Sussex Regiment and so on), RAF unit (617 Squadron, RAF Tangmere) or naval ship or base (HMS *Victoria*, HMS *Terror*) because records are often created or arranged by individual units.

Starting Out

Both the Imperial War Museum (IWM) and The National Archives (TNA) have leaflets that can be downloaded, providing basic guidance about starting military genealogical research. There are dozens in TNA's Research Guide series, which concentrates almost exclusively on sources at Kew (www.nationalarchives.gov.uk/catalogue), while IWM's are largely about the twentieth century including sources at the Museum, Kew and elsewhere (www.iwm.org.uk/server/show/nav.00100a). Other museums may well also produce guidance for family historians as well. The (Canadian) Global Gazette at http://globalgenealogy.com/countries/england/global-gazette-england.htm, and the Genuki (Genealogy United Kingdom and Ireland) at www.genuki.org.uk/big/MilitaryRecords.html, both have some useful introductory essays.

Several professional researchers also provide pages of guidance, including:

- www.barnettresearch.freeserve.co.uk – Len Barnett – maritime and naval history.

- www.rfc-rnas-raf-register.org.uk – David J Barnes – Boer and First World War. Offers a speciality service in identifying military photographs.

- www.militaryarchiveresearch.com – Dr Steven Blank – general military genealogy.

- www.militaryresearchon.com – Jonathan Collins – general military genealogy, specialises in medals.

- www.researchthepast.com – Hannah Cunliffe – maritime research.

- www.searcher-na.co.uk – Bob O'Hara – general military genealogy.

- www.na-searcher.co.uk – Richard Robinson – military aviation.

- www.angelfire.com/ga/BobSanders – Bob Sanders – naval and Merchant Navy research.

- www.btinternet.com/~prosearch – Tom Tulloch-Marshall – First World War.

- www.btinternet.com/%7Elawrence.woodcock – Lawrence Woodcock – all three services.

An excellent introduction to tracing soldiers and Army officers is provided by the Army Museum Ogilby Trust at www.armymuseums.org.uk/ ancestor.htm. Gavin Jones's naval advice at http://home.swipnet.se/~w-11 578/research.htm is rather dated, but is still useful, particularly for the pre-twentieth-century material. I especially liked his definition of research as being 'the process of going up alleys to see if they are blind'.

If you want to trace service personnel who served after the end of the First World War (or their medals), you should be aware that their service records are still with the Ministry of Defence, although they can be seen for a fee, normally £30, this may be waived for servicemen themselves or their immediate next of kin. The Service Personnel and Veterans Agency provide useful pages about getting hold of these records at: www.veterans-uk.info, as do a number of regimental museums.

Links to hundreds of British military genealogy websites can be found at www.cyndislist.com/miluk.htm.

Mailing Lists

Websites may not always be much help in providing answers to particular problems once you start researching an individual soldier. An alternative lies in the various on-line discussion forums, which are ideal places to ask questions or learn from the experience of others. For example, I belong to a First World War mailing list, which has a constant stream of requests for help with members' research, which are patiently answered by other list members.

The best list of genealogical mailing lists is provided by GENUKI (www.genuki.org.uk/indexes/MailingLists.html). A guide to mailing lists worldwide is at www.rootsweb.com/~jfuller/gen_mail_wars.html.

There are also lists for military history rather than military genealogy, which may be of help in understanding historical or regimental background. They are much more difficult to track down and are listed in the relevant chapter below.

Websites That Charge

An increasing proportion of the records at The National Archives and other places are being digitised and the resulting images made available online for a fee. Most of the larger companies allow you to either subscribe (that is, pay for a year's access or a shorter period if you wish) or buy a voucher giving you access to a certain number of images for a particular amount (normally units of £5). Family history magazines occasionally give away free vouchers, so keep a look-out.

In almost all cases it is possible to use the index for free, which should give enough data to confirm that you have probably tracked down the right person. You then pay to access the complete record.

At the time of writing the most comprehensive of the services (at least for research of individual servicemen) is The National Archives' Documents Online at www.nationalarchives/documentsonline. Among other resources it includes:

- Prerogative Court of Canterbury wills to 1858 (includes many wills made by Army and Navy officers and surprisingly often by seamen and ordinary soldiers).

- Registers of winners of the Victoria Cross, 1856–1945.

- Service records for RN seamen, 1873–1923.

- Medal Index Cards for the Army and RAF, 1914–1919 (these cards give brief details of every man, woman and officer who served overseas during the First World War).

- Women's Auxiliary Army Corps service records 1917–1918.

- Royal Naval Division service records, First World War.

- Interviews with returning prisoners of war, First World War.

- A small collection of war diaries, First World War.
  Medal rolls for merchant seamen, Second World War.

It is unlikely that any more major series of military documents will be added in the foreseeable future, but smaller collections and odd items will be including seamen's wills in series ADM 48 and RAF combat reports in AIR 50, so it is worth checking occasionally.

There are two major commercial companies in the field – Ancestry.co.uk and FindMyPast. Both offer indexes to English and Welsh birth, marriage and death registers from 1837 and censuses between 1841 and 1901. Indeed neither source can be entirely neglected because they often list servicemen and may supply details, such as the regiment or ship they were serving with. As regards unique holdings for military historians, Ancestry (www.ancestry.co.uk) has:

- First World War soldiers' documents (incomplete at time of writing, but should all be online by the end of 2008).

- Commissioned Sea Officers of the Royal Navy 1660–1815 (taken from the book of the same name).

- British and German Deserters, Dischargees, and POWs Who May Have Remained in Canada and the USA, 1774–1783 (taken from the book of the same name).

FindMyPast (www.findmypast.com) has:

- Birth, marriage and death records for the Armed Forces (mainly Army) 1761–1994.

- Peninsular Medal Roll, 1808–1814.

- Soldiers died in the Great War.

- National Roll of Honour, 1914–1919 (very incomplete and including civilians).

- Army Roll of Honour, 1939–1945.

- A variety of miscellaneous scanned indexes, rolls of honour, and Army and Navy lists.

- Outward bound passenger lists 1890–1960 (mainly for civilians, but occasionally include officers and other ranks being sent to serve in India and other places overseas).

In addition, there are a number of smaller websites that contain military genealogical material:

www.familyrelatives.com – records of births, marriages and deaths of servicemen (similar to those with FindMyPast), as well the major BMD indexes and censuses. It has a loyal fan base of subscribers who claim that the site is easier to use.

The site from the Naval and Military Press – www.military-genealogy.co.uk has a variety of databases for the two world wars. At present they are: Soldiers Died in the Great War; National Roll of Honour; Royal Naval Division (First World War); De Revigny's roll of honour for officers, 1914–1918; and the Army Roll of Honour 1939–1945.

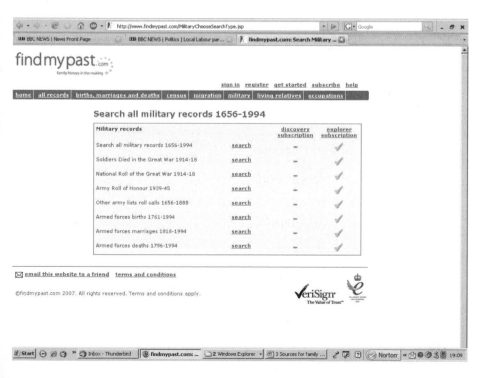

www.theoriginalrecord.com – has scans of many Army and Navy Lists and other books containing details of military personnel.

www.scotlandspeople.gov.uk – has birth, marriage, death records and census material for Scotland. Data to be added shortly are the 'minor records' including registers of births, marriages and deaths of Scottish soldiers across the globe.

www.wartimesindex.co.uk supplies details of deaths mainly of officers between 1854 and 1902 from *The Times, London Gazette* and other sources. However, it is possible to get free access to *The Times* online and *London Gazette* at your local library at www.gazettes-online.co.uk.

Actual birth, marriage and death certificates in England and Wales (rather than the registers as at present) will be made available online probably during the spring and summer of 2008. Details are at www.gro.gov.uk.

The 1911 census will be made available online during 2009. The URL is not known at time of writing, but no doubt there will exhaustive publicity around its launch.

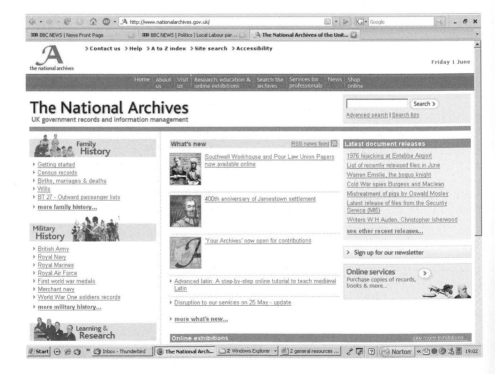

At present, TNA is tendering for licences to digitise and scan pre-First World War service records, some Irish military material as well as officers' service records between 1914 and 1920. It is likely that these will be available online by 2010. The genealogical press and TNA's own website will keep you informed of how this is progressing.

Free Resources

There are however lots of resources online which are free, although inevitably the topics they cover are often patchy. The *London Gazette* is the government's own newspaper (published since 1665) containing official notices, including the promotions of officers, awards of medals and printed despatches from commanders. The Gazette between 1752 and 1979 has been digitised and is available in a fully searchable form at www.gazettes-online.co.uk. It helps if you know the approximate date of an entry.

The online catalogue of The National Archives (www.nationalarchives.gov.uk/catalogue) contains brief details of every soldier who survived to receive a pension between about 1760 and 1854, as well as for Army officers between 1914 and 1918. When searching the catalogue, type the person's name (often just the surname will do) into the subject box and WO 97 (for soldiers' documents) and WO 339 or WO 373 (for officers) in the Department/series code box. www.geocities.com/crawford_file/index.html contains histories of some servicemen (Army, RAF and Navy) with the surname Crawford.

Medals

The first campaign medals issued by the government (with the exception of the one awarded to men who took part at Waterloo) were the Naval and Military general service medals issued in the 1840s for men who had served in the Napoleonic Wars. The most famous gallantry medals are the Victoria and George crosses, established in 1856 and 1940 respectively, but there are a number of others, most of which were set up in the later nineteenth century. Winners of gallantry awards are 'gazetted' – that is, details of the award are published in the *London Gazette* (www.gazettes-online.co.uk).

There are many medal websites, with a fair overlap in subject matter, generally catering for medal collectors, including:

www.diggerhistory.info/pages-medals/00-medals-cat-index.htm is a well laid-out introductory site dedicated to medals and medal holders, with an Australian bias, although as until the 1960s the medals were nearly identical it does not matter.

www.medals.org.uk is a general site devoted to the medals of the world, with images of medals and ribbons. Rather more impressive, and definitely one for the enthusiast, is www.jeanpaulleblanc.com, with lots of resources about medals and their holders with links and news stories about medals.

If you are trying to identify a badge www.militarybadges.org.uk/badges/badgestart.htm is a good place to start, although it is not really indexed by unit, or by type of badge, so it involves a great deal of scrolling.

www.northeastmedals.co.uk is an excellent website from a medal dealer in Northumberland with clear images and descriptions of the medals on sale – which is useful guide to prices. There is also additional information, such as a list of the men who lost their lives at Jutland.

The Orders and Medals Research Society has a pretty basic website at www.omrs.org.uk. If you are an enthusiastic medal collector then you should join.

www.gc-database.co.uk is a superb site devoted to the George Cross and holders of the medals. www.angelfire.com/va/violetteszabo/georgecross.html – more pages on George Cross including some audio clips.

As might be expected there are a number of sites devoted to the Victoria Cross and winners of the medal. The Victoria Cross Society – www.victoriacrosssociety.com – exists to encourage research into the medal and its holders. www.victoriacross.org.uk has details of all VC winners and lists where they are buried.

If you are researching Second World War medals http://users.skynet.be/hendrik/index.html has descriptions and illustrations of medals awarded by all sides.

Tracing Sailors

For general advice about research into RN officers and seamen www.mariners-l.co.uk/UKRoyalNavyIndex.html is a good bet. There are also pages about shore stations (which confusingly to non-mariners are given ships' names) and where they were located and a history of the Royal Naval School at Greenwich. A few examples of transcripts of individuals' service records (mainly for the late nineteenth-century Navy) are at www.rimell.u-net.com.

www.pbenyon.plus.com/Naval.html is an attractive miscellanea of a site generally reprinting pages from newspapers and books, such as the Navy List, about the Navy from about 1770 to 1930, with lots of names, particularly of officers. It is also simply laid out.

An index to all Royal Navy officers between 1793 and 1815 taken from the
Navy Lists of the period can be found at
www.ageofnelson.org/NavyList/index.html. Only basic information is
given, but if you want to know more you can buy a CD.

A list of Irish officers in the Royal Navy during the Napoleonic wars, with
brief biographical details compiled by Anthony Gary Brown, is at
www.agbfinebooks.com/Publications/Irish/Irish%20Web.htm

A list of 1,640 men and officers who were at Trafalgar (based on a medal roll)
is at www.genuki.org.uk/big/eng/Trafalgar. Much more complete is the
fully searchable Trafalgar Roll to over 18,000 men (and one woman) who
were present at the battle, taken from musters and other records at The
National Archives at www.nationalarchives.gov.uk/trafalgarancestors.
There is also an on-line exhibition devoted to the Battle.

www.agbfinebooks.com/Publications/Marshall/MarshallWeb.htm contains
an Index to the Entries in Lieutenant John Marshall's 'Royal Naval
Biography', which was originally published in 12 volumes, in London,
between 1823 and 1835. The material largely describes officers who had
served during the Napoleonic wars. Marshall has been republished by the
Naval and Military Press and so may be available in local studies and family
history libraries.

www.pbenyon1.plus.com/Nbd/Index.html has lists of officers between 1844
and 1879 taken from the Navy Lists. It is by no means complete, but
indicative of the sort of information which can be found in the Lists.

The major naval battle of the First World War was at Jutland.
www.northeastmedals.co.uk/britishguide/jutland/jellicoe_dispatch_
1916.htm contains a list of men killed there.

www.unithistories.com/officers/RNVR_officersA.html contains an
alphabetical list of all Royal Naval Volunteer Research (RNVR) officers with
brief details of their service during the Second World War. There are also
some photographs of individuals.

Local History

A greatly neglected aspect of both military and local history is the overlap
between the two disciplines. Yet every county and almost every town had a
militia unit, made up of part-time soldiers recruited locally. Many places had
a regimental depot, and in a few places – Aldershot, Plymouth and
Portsmouth for example – the military presence was the mainstay of the
economy, and has left a physical record behind.

The English Heritage's View Finder database at http://viewfinder.english-heritage.org.uk contains thousands of old photographs. You can search it for images of forts and barracks around the country.

One of the most useful of the village and town sites is www.burtonlatimer.info/war/warindex.html, which has lots of pages from the English Civil War to the Second World War regarding Burton Latimer, Northants., and the men of that area.

There are pages about the military history of the Isle of Man at www.isle-of-man.com/manxnotebook/history/index.htm, with much else besides.

www.juroch.demon.co.uk/kentvad.htm tells the history of Kent Voluntary Aid Detachments during the First World War, with lists of auxiliary hospitals in the county and across the UK. It is best read in Internet Explorer.

www.cyber-heritage.co.uk is a portmanteau site, that is one devoted to a large number of different subject, in this case related to the history of Plymouth and surrounding area, with an emphasis on the military side of things.

www.btinternet.com/%7Ejames.fanning/westcalder1/index.html explores the experiences of West Calder near Edinburgh during the First World War, with a link to a site devoted to the village's war memorial.

www.royal-arsenal.com provides a brief history and description of the Royal Artillery site at Woolwich. It claims to be a temporary site, but has been up since the end of 2002.

There are a number pages devoted to the military history of Yorkshire at www.yorkshirehistory.com, including the Siege of Hull during the Civil War, and the performance of the county's regiments at the Battle of Waterloo.

Many coastal towns and districts have coastal fortifications of one kind or another. There are several excellent websites listing them:

- Subterranea Britannica is an organisation that investigates underground structures of all kinds. Their excellent website at www.subbrit.org.uk includes a directory to military diggings of all kinds, including Cold War bunkers.

- During the Napoleonic wars a large number of Martello towers were built to protect the British coast. Much about them can be found at the detailed and attractive www.martello-towers.co.uk.

- The same webmaster also runs www.pillbox.org.uk, which lists and describes pillboxes and other structures hurriedly built in the summer of 1940 to defend strong points in case of German invasion.

- The Coal House Fort is a restored mid-Victorian fort at Tilbury, Essex, whose website is http://coalhousefort-gallery.com.

Finally, there is one military artefact that every city, town and village has: the war memorial. This and the related rolls of honour are discussed in the next section.

Further Reading

There are no bibliographies for other sections, because there seems little point. However, if you are tracing military ancestors or individual servicemen it is worth buying one or more of the guides listed below, because they contain important and useful information not available online (or, if it is, it is hard to find):

- Simon Fowler, *Tracing Army Ancestors* (Pen and Sword, 2006)

- Simon Fowler, *Tracing First World War Ancestors* (Countryside Books, 2003 new edition due 2008)

- Simon Fowler, *Tracing Second World War Ancestors* (Countryside Books, 2006)

- Bruno Pappalardo, *Tracing Your Naval Ancestors* (The National Archives, 2003)

- William Spencer, *Army Service Records of the First World War* (The National Archives, 2001)

- William Spencer, *Family History in the Wars* (The National Archives, 2007)

- William Spencer, *Medals: the Researcher's Guide* (The National Archives, 2006)

- Phil Tomaselli, *Tracing RAF Ancestors* (Pen and Sword, 2007)

In addition, the Imperial War Museum has published a series of *Tracing your Family History* books on the Army, Royal Navy and Royal Air Force, second editions of which were published in 2005. They are mainly useful for the twentieth century.

Chapter 3

WAR MEMORIALS AND ROLLS OF HONOUR

Considering the current obsession with internet-based genealogy, it is unsurprising that many sites exist relating to war memorials. Often, the webmaster or organisation provides a list of names plus information about each individual.

The first memorials to the fallen were generally for officers and placed in parish churches. They began to appear in the mid-eighteenth century and are still being erected today. Genealogists refer to these as monumental inscriptions (MIs), and many family history societies have compiled indexes to, and lists of, inscriptions found in local churches and churchyards. Unfortunately, relatively few lists have appeared online, but a few can be found at Family History Online at www.familyhistoryonline.org.uk. The National Archive of Memorial Inscriptions (NAOMI) is a nationwide project to provide a single list of MIs. Details and a searchable database can be found at www.memorialinscriptions.org.uk, although at present it only relates to Norfolk.

More formal memorials and monuments to groups of men and officers who lost their lives in the service of their regiment and country began to be erected after the Napoleonic Wars. Some 53,000 such memorials from the late eighteenth century to the present day have been identified by the UK National Inventory of War Memorials and are listed at www.ukniwm.org.uk. The website contains a database searchable by campaign, place or even type of memorial. What it does not provide are the names found on memorials, although names on memorials dedicated to individuals or small groups of people are often included.

National Records

The National Maritime Museum maintains a database of Maritime Memorials at www.nmm.ac.uk/memorials, which contains records of over 4,000 church, cemetery and public memorials to seafarers and victims of

maritime disasters, mainly in Britain, but some overseas ones are included as well. The earliest so far identified is for George Beeston, who died in 1601, having served against the Spanish Armada, and who is commemorated at St Boniface, Bunbury, in Cheshire. As well as searching by campaign and place, it is also possible to search by how the person(s) commemorated died, manner of death (such as 'execution' or 'killed by natives') and theme (e.g. 'piracy').

If you are interested in Army and Navy officers who died in the service of their country between about 1750 and 1950 then an incomplete database is at www.redcoat.info/memindex3.htm. It is particularly good for men who died in India. A similar site for other ranks can be found at www.angelfire.com/mp/memorials/memindz1.htm. As well as the eighteenth- and nineteenth-century records, there are rolls for men who died during the Malayan Emergency, the Korean War and in Northern Ireland.

Many Irishmen fought in the British Army, even after Southern Ireland (Éire) won independence in 1922. www.irishwarmemorials.ie is a superb site listing war memorials in Ireland north and south. It includes photographs of each memorial, the text of all inscriptions, and details of the site of the memorial. A database of all of those named allows a search for individual persons, with links to the photographs of the memorials. Visitors to the site are encouraged to add information about the individuals commemorated and supply additional photographs of memorials.

The National Memorial Arboretum, in a former gravel pit in Staffordshire, has a number of memorials provided by various associations to men who lost their lives in a number of campaigns. The best known is for those 'Shot at Dawn' during the First World War. More details about the Arboretum can be found at www.memorialtreesuk.org.uk.

The War Memorials Trust (formerly the Friends of War Memorials) was set up to preserve war memorials across the United Kingdom. Details of their work can be found at www.warmemorials.org.

The British War Memorial Project at www.britishwargraves.org.uk offers a handsome virtual war memorial to service personnel from 1914 to the present day – including those killed in recent conflicts and peacekeeping operations. The site claims that its grave and memorial photo archive is the largest of its kind in the world, and is continually updated by a global volunteer network. You can search the database by the name of the deceased or by cemetery.

In November 2002 the Memorial Gates Trust erected a memorial near Buckingham Palace to the men from the Indian subcontinent (as well as Africa and the Caribbean) who lost their lives during the two world wars. The website at www.mgtrust.org also includes provides details of the battles they fought in.

The custodian of war memorials and cemeteries for men and women who laid down their lives during the two world wars is the Commonwealth War Graves Commission. Established by Royal Charter in 1917, the Commission pays tribute to the 1,700,000 service personnel from the Commonwealth forces who died in the two world wars. Since its inception, the Commission has constructed 2,500 war cemeteries and plots, erecting headstones over graves and, in instances where the remains are missing, inscribing the names of the dead on permanent memorials. Over 1 million casualties are now commemorated at military and civil sites in some 150 countries. Not least of its achievements is a magnificent website at www.cwgc.org, listing not only all the men and women who died in the service of 'King and Empire' but also all the cemeteries around the world in which they lie, with brief histories of how they came to be established and directions of how to get there.

Inevitably the Commission has its critics, and there are claims that it has left off 15,000 men from its registers. A site that is campaigning for these omissions – particularly for men from the Royal Naval Division during the First World War – to be rectified can be found at http://cwgc.co.uk.

Local And Regional Surveys

Many names from war memorials across Britain can be found at www.roll-of-honour.com. It is by no means complete and there is a degree of overlap with some of the official sites described above. It is probably most useful for

minor conflicts, such the Boer War, and the post-war conflicts, including a list of service personnel who died during the Northern Irish 'Troubles'.

The Association of Jewish Ex-servicemen at www.ajex.org.uk provides a roll of honour for Jews in the Army during the two world wars, as well as information about the Jewish Military Museum in Hendon.

The North-East War Memorials Project (www.newmp.org.uk) contains information about war memorials, of whatever type, located in Northumberland, Newcastle-on-Tyne and County Durham, as defined by the pre-1974 boundaries. You can search by place or name. The entry for each memorial includes a full transcription of any inscription and the individuals commemorated on it.

www.geocities.com/abbertonroh describes the men who lost their lives during the two world wars from the villages of Abberton and Langenhoe near Colchester.

www.carlscam.com/memo.htm contains photographs of memorials from Napoleonic Wars onwards, generally with some connection to Cheshire.

http://web.ukonline.co.uk/flight/warmemorial.html contains names from war memorials mainly for the two world wars which can be found in Gloucestershire. It is arranged by parish rather than by name and contains transcripts of memorials with brief biographical information about each man found on them.

www.isle-of-wight-memorials.org.uk lists war and civic memorials on the Isle of Wight.

With its longstanding naval presence, Portsmouth has many more war memorials than for other towns of similar size. They are listed, described and transcribed in an attractive site at www.memorials.inportsmouth.co.uk.

First World War Memorials

The vast majority of memorials commemorate the men who fell during the First World War. They were established as physical evidence of the immense outpouring of grief that occurred as the casualty lists mounted in 1915. Initially, street shrines appeared in working-class districts of London and other large cities, but the Imperial (later Commonwealth) War Graves Commission was appointed in 1917 to ensure that the sacrifice of the fallen was appropriately commemorated, and finally the Cenotaph was unveiled on Armistice Day 1920. In the years after the Armistice every town and village built their own war memorials, most of which can still be seen. Schools, trades and church congregations also unveiled their own memorials – I remember coming across a plaque at the Royal Hospital Richmond, dedicated to the milkmen of the Thames Valley who never returned to their rounds.

A few years ago Channel 4 screened an excellent series telling the stories behind a few war memorials. One by-product was the Lost Generations website www.channel4.com/history/microsites/L/lostgeneration/index.html, which was originally intended to include a database of individual names on war memorials. As it turned out, only very few memorials were actually transcribed and the site is now largely a general history of the war for schools.

www.aftermathww1.com/index.asp offers an introduction to the mourning and grief that led to the establishment of the war memorials. Unfortunately the site needs updating.

www.wargravephotoservice.20m.com is a commercial service offering photographs of individual war graves.

All 940 war cemeteries with 40 burials and above have been visited and photographed by Brent Whittam and Terry Heard in recent years, whose pictures can be found at www.ww1cemeteries.com. The site also contains photographs of many military cemeteries and memorials from around the world, including an increasing number of British ones, such as the memorial to the sacrifices of British women at Upavon, Wiltshire.

www.snwm.org/website/history/index.html provides a detailed history of the Scottish National Memorial, which is to be found high above Edinburgh.

http://scottishmonument.be/scottishmonument.htm relates to the campaign to dedicate a new memorial to the Scots who fell in Flanders. It uses Flash graphics, so may not be suitable for every computer, and there is a mawkish soundtrack as well, although this can be switched off.

First World War Memorials – Local

War memorials are of course almost all listed on the UK National Inventory of War Memorials (see above). Even so, there are dozens of websites describing local memorials and the men who are honoured on them. A slightly dated list can be found in the two volumes of Stuart Raymond's *War Memorials on the Web* (FFHS, 2004), which can be ordered from the author at www.samjraymond.btinternet.co.uk. Here are some of the most interesting:

- www.bidfordwarmemorial.co.uk for the men from the idyllic Warwickshire village of Bidford on Avon.

- http://fp.underw.f9.co.uk/bucksrems/index.htm is the website of 'Buckinghamshire Remembers' for the men who made the ultimate sacrifice from the county. It contains a fully searchable database of local men who did not return.

- www.burnleyinthegreatwar.info is about Burnley in the war and the men who went away to fight. At the heart are descriptions and information about many of the town's memorials.

- www.hamm25.freeserve.co.uk an incomplete guide to the war memorials of the Calderdale area of Yorkshire.

- http://members.aol.com/John1hartley/html an attractive sire for Cheadle and Gatley war memorials near Stockport, Cheshire. It includes men who died in both world wars.

The model for all other sites on war memorials must be www.remembering.org.uk, which is a detailed look at the men who appear on the memorials and roll of honours for Cheltenham. There is even a page about the men who died after the armistice (of wounds contracted during the war) but who are not commemorated on the town's war memorials.

Transcriptions of war memorials for Clevedon, Somerset and the area around it can be found at www.curme.co.uk/clvdnndx.htm. The town unusually has

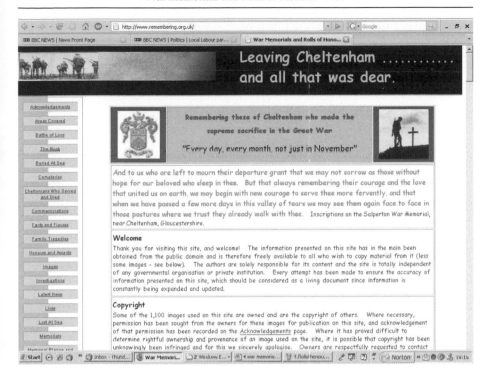

a 'peace memorial', which commemorates men from the town who fell during the Boer War.

www.camulos.com/war has transcripts of war memorials around Colchester and district.

http://homepage.ntlworld.com/howard.martin has detailed biographies for some of the men who appear on the war memorial at Cartmel in Cumbria.

An excellent and detailed site about men from Derbyshire who served in the war is at /www.derbyshirelads.uwclub.net, with lists of names from war memorials in the county.

www.goring1941.freeserve.co.uk/seewmami.html contains details of a project to transcribe war memorials and rolls of honour for South East Essex. No data is found on the site itself, but will be given to enquirers by the webmaster.

Details and photographs of a small number of unusual war memorials in central London are at www.resthepast.co.uk/warmemorials/londonmemorials.html.

Hidden away on the website of the Department for Trade and Industry, at www.dti.gov.uk/about/aboutus/warmemorial/index.html, there is a roll of honour for the men from the Board of Trade who died during the war. There are also lists of men from the department who served.

www.islandhistory.org.uk is a local history site for the Isle of Dogs, with a scan of the roll of honour for men from St Luke's, Millwall. There are other interesting pages about the area during the two world wars.

Manchester and Lancashire FHS have transcribed a number of war memorials for local companies at www.mlfhs.org.uk.

www.readingremembrancetrust.co.uk describes the men from the Berkshire town who failed to return.

www.users.globalnet.co.uk/~shelvey has details of all the men from Rutland who are commemorated on the county's war memorials. It is arranged by parish.

www.sittingbourneremembers.uni.cc is a detailed site devoted to the men on the war memorials in and around Sittingbourne and Milton Regis, Kent.

http://homepage.ntlworld.com/bandl.danby/Skelton1918_1919.html describes the places where men from Skelton in Cleveland are commemorated, both in Skelton itself and in Belgium.

www.slaidburn.org.uk/ww1.htm for men from Slaidburn, in the Forest of Bowland, who fell during the First World War. There are also similar pages for the 1939-1945 War.

www.stock.org.uk/sub-index/war-memorials.htm has details of memorials in Stock and neighbouring parishes in Essex for both world wars.

Biographies of men on Stockport's war memorial can be found at www.stockport1914–1918.co.uk. There is also a page relating to war memorials on the Western Front, which commemorate those who have no known grave.

www.suffolk.gov.uk/LeisureAndCulture/LocalHistoryAndHeritage/ SuffolkRecordOffice/Collections/RollOfHonour.htm list men from Suffolk who did not return.

The story of the men from the small Cambridgeshire village of Swavesey is told at www.curme.co.uk. The site also has details of members of Lloyds Bank who appear on the company's war memorial.

www.tellthemofus.org.uk is the website of a recent book about the men from Swindon who fell during the First World War. It contains some interesting photos.

www.smilodon.plus.com/WarMems is mainly for villages in the Welsh marches.

The war memorials of Wolverhampton and district are described at www.warmem.pwp.blueyonder.co.uk.

Second World War Memorials

A number of the memorials and rolls of honour for the First World War described above include lists of men who died during the second 'war to end war'. There are, however, a few sites specifically for the Second World War including:

- Although it largely duplicates the efforts of the Commonwealth War Graves Commission, Second World War Cemeteries at www.ww2cemeteries.co.uk is attempting to record and photograph all the Second World War cemeteries graves and memorials, not just in the UK but across the world. At present it is focused on Europe, but there are also pages offering advice about researching men who fought in the war.

- An index to the Civilian War Dead Roll of Honour compiled by the Commonwealth War Graves Commission for Durham, Northumberland and Yorkshire can be found at www.genuki.org.uk/big/eng/Indexes/NE_WarDead. It also includes a description of problems in using the Roll. It is a pity that there isn't a similar resource for other counties or regions.

- After the war an Army Roll of Honour was compiled by the War Office. The original is now at The National Archives. It is available online at www.military-genealogy.com, from where details of individuals can be downloaded for a fee.

- www.petrowilliamus.co.uk/kranji/pictures/kranji has details of the Kranji war memorial and cemetery in Singapore.

- www.airscene.org/monument/home.htm relates to the RAF and Allied Air Forces Memorial in Plymouth, including brief histories of the RAF and Allied air forces and lists of VC and GC winners, although there are no names on the monument itself.

- www.goring1941.freeserve.co.uk contains lists of Essex people killed during the war, largely taken from war memorials.

- A list of Essex policemen who lost their lives during the war is at www.essex.police.uk/memorial/ww2.htm.

Non-British War Memorials

The American Battle Monuments Commission website at www.abmc.gov/home.php includes an incomplete database relating to casualties of the two world wars and Korea, together with their last resting places.

http://www.ww1-ww2-commemorations.com/index.htm is a Belgian site about the dead of the two world wars, providing a useful calendar of commemorations in Belgium, Britain and other countries.

Lists of Belgian war graves during the two world wars can be found at http://users.pandora.be/ABL1914/BWG/BWGfront.htm. It is written in Dutch but is reasonably easy to work out.

www.wo1.be/eng/mainnav.html contains links to pages and databases about Belgian and French soldiers killed in Belgium, as well as German, American and Commonwealth sites.

The Canadian Virtual War Memory, www.vac-acc.gc.ca/remembers/sub.cfm?source=collections/virtualmem, has details of the 116,000 Canadians who lost their lives in wars fought by the country.

www.vac-acc.gc.ca/remembers/sub.cfm?source=memorials/cbmr/wall_stone_display is devoted to the Vimy Ridge memorial, with a 3D tour and lists of names of the Canadians who appear on it.

www.mapleleaflegacy.org intends to photograph each of these men's graves – the Australian equivalent is www.australianwargraves.org, the British and New Zealand is at www.britishwargraves.org.uk, and the South African www.southafricawargraves.org.

http://www.stemnet.nf.ca/monuments/index.htm has photographs and details of war memorials across Canada.

http://wonderstrand.com/memorial/project.html is an on-line memorial to the men from Labrador who fought in the two world wars and Korea.

www.memoiredeshommes.sga.defense.gouv.fr/index_en.htm is the official database for French soldiers who died during the First World War and other wars of the twentieth century.

The German war graves commission can be found at www.volksbund.de. The site is in German, but an article in English about its work and history is at www.greatwar.co.uk/westfront/cemeteries/gecemies.htm.

The Dutch equivalent is at www.ogs.nl. Most of the site is in Dutch, but there is a PDF leaflet on war graves in Indonesia in English.

Of all the Allied nations, New Zealand suffered the greatest losses, proportionally speaking, during the First World War. www.nzhistory.net.nz/?q=node/392 contains photographs and details of 450 war memorials erected in New Zealand after 1918.

Chapter 4

MILITARY MUSEUMS

There are a surprisingly large number of military and aviation museums scattered across the United Kingdom. They vary considerably from slick and lavish national institutions to small rooms maintained by a volunteer or two. Personally, I prefer the smaller establishments because on the whole they offer a more authentic experience – the larger museums have a tendency to dumb down their exhibits for schoolchildren, who presumably make up the vast majority of visitors, and it hurts my brain having to read exhibit captions written for eight-year-olds.

Museums have trouble knowing what to do with their websites. At their simplest they are nothing more than an on-line brochure. Most, however, try to offer more, particularly for schools and the enthusiast. Some have put images of at least part of their collections online, or offer a 'virtual tour' (usually photos of the galleries or exhibits), but websites can't replicate the actual experience of visiting.

Finding Museums

It can be hard to find out about museums, although most now have websites. Many of the larger ones are involved in local tourism and may thus be found on tourist sites, such as www.aboutbritain.com/default.htm, or sites with a more historical bent, such as www.history.uk.com – actually a monthly newsletter, to which it is well worth subscribing. Also of interest is the '24-hour museum' (www.24hourmuseum.org.uk), which combines news stories from museums plus details of locations, opening hours etc.

You might also try www.warmuseums.nl, which is a guide to military museums across Europe. As well as the usual information about opening hours, location etc., it offers a review in slightly fractured English. The site is by no means comprehensive, but if you are going to the Continent on holiday and are looking for a museum to visit when it is wet, this is a good place to start, particularly as it lists some of the less usual lesser known places.

An online phenomenon is the 'feedback' or 'review' site, whereby users post their experiences of hotels, attractions and the like. The largest such site is www.tripadvisor.com, which does include reviews of the larger military attractions, although it has to be said that the comments regarding the RAF and Imperial War museums were hardly revealing. There does not seem to be one specifically dedicated to museums or heritage attractions.

National Museums

Undoubtedly, the most important museum of military history is the Imperial War Museum, although it specialises in the period after 1914. As well as the main building near the Elephant and Castle in south London, there are branches at Duxford near Cambridge (for military aviation), Manchester (IWM North), as well as the Churchill Museum, Cabinet War Rooms and HMS *Belfast* elsewhere in London. All are well worth visiting. The main Museum and IWM North are free, but charges are levied for the other branches. Visitor information, and much else beside, can be found on the clear and uncluttered website www.iwm.org.uk, although, if your eyesight is poor, you may find it difficult to read the text as the type size is quite small.

There is also a wide range of on-line exhibitions (click on 'online resources' on the home page) that offer a glimpse into the IWM and its collections. Many were put up to accompany exhibitions in the Museum, while others just seem to be the results of trying out new technology and techniques.

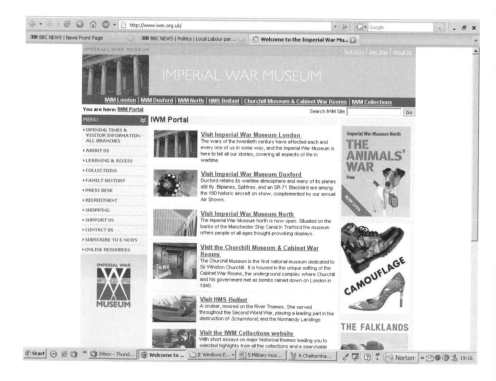

Some themes are well known, such as the war poets of the First World War, while others are more obscure, such as the one devoted to Eric Ravilious, an official war artist before his untimely early death in 1942 in an air accident off Iceland, or the one about the survivors of the SS *Anglo-Saxon*, which was sunk by the German armed merchantmen *Widder* in August 1940. At the time of writing there were over 30 such exhibitions to explore.

The other national museum to really embrace cyberspace is the National Maritime Museum in Greenwich at www.nmm.ac.uk. The Museum also includes the neighbouring Queen's House and Royal Observatory, and makes a splendid day out, even if you are seasick at the sight of a canoe. And at Falmouth there is an out-station of National Maritime Museum Cornwall (www.nmmc.co.uk).

As well as the usual information for visitors there is an on-line catalogue and images of 9,000 items from the collections. It is possible to buy copies of an image for personal use, but it is rather expensive.

Cunningly hidden are a number of on-line exhibitions – I particularly liked the one about Admiral Nelson. You need to click on 'What's on' on the homepage and then on 'online features'. The address is www.nmm.ac.uk/server/show/nav.005001004.

There are also links to Maritime Art Greenwich, which is a database of the Museum's art collection (www.nmm.ac.uk/mag) and the PORT Information gateway at www.port.nmm.ac.uk, which is an important resource for researchers into maritime and naval history.

Less useful are the sites for the National Army, Royal Naval and RAF museums.

The National Army Museum, next door to Chelsea Royal Hospital, tells the story of the British Army since its foundation in the 1660s. The website at www.national-army-museum.ac.uk, which has recently been redesigned and improved, gives all the information you would expect, but there is only the briefest description of the collections and no on-line catalogue, although one is promised by the end of 2007. There are, however, a number of on-line exhibitions, which are easy to find from the homepage, although they are marred because most of the images are too small to view with ease, and you can't click on them to enlarge them.

The Royal Naval Museum can be found in the heart of the Naval Dockyard at Portsmouth. The disappointing website at www.royalnavalmuseum.org is functional, with descriptions of the galleries. The only on-line exhibition at the time of writing was on the Dreadnaught class of battleships. However, there are well-hidden information sheets and, more importantly, an on-line catalogue to the archives held by the museum (click on 'Research', then on 'Research Online').

The RAF Museum is located in a windswept part of Hendon, North London (www.rafmuseum.org.uk). There is an outstation at RAF Cosford in Shropshire (www.rafmuseum.org.uk/cosford/index.cfm). It was founded to tell the story of the Royal Air Force. The website contains the usual information about opening hours, plus a little about the research collections and brief descriptions of the aircraft, engines and motor vehicles in their collections. There is also an on-line catalogue, called Navigator (http://navigator.rafmuseum.org), with sections on aircraft, flying boats, vehicles, Cold War missiles, Bristol engines and, oddly, operations rooms. Many of the photographs are hard to see because they are very dark: a measure, perhaps, to stop people from using them without paying reproduction or copyright fees?

In addition, the Royal Armouries at www.royalarmouries.org has a rather disappointing site aimed very much at the visitor rather than the enthusiast. The Armouries run museums at the Tower of London and in Leeds, with a comprehensive collection of guns, armour and armaments of all kind. However, you can search the library catalogue and buy scans of items from it, but there are few images of armour and the like.

Museums in Scotland

If you are interested in the Scottish regiments then www.cabarfeidh.com/other_regiments.htm is a good place to start, because if offers links to local regimental museums. It will also play the appropriate regimental marches on bagpipes.

The Scottish National War Museum in Edinburgh Castle (formerly the Scottish United Services Museum) is an essential place for people interested in the Highlanders and Lowlanders, although you won't necessarily gain this feeling from a visit to their website at www.nms.ac.uk/warmuseumhomepage.aspx.

More satisfactory is the Scots at War website, www.scotsatwar.org.uk, which looks at the experiences of Scottish men in uniform, with photographs and memories of veterans.

www.argylls.co.uk is the regimental museum of the Argyll and Sutherland Highlanders at Stirling Castle. It includes a list of officers and other ranks in the regiment in 1794.

www.gordonhighlanders.com is the regimental museum (and commemorative gardens) of the Gordon Highlanders in Aberdeen.

www.kosb.co.uk/museum is the rather disappointing site for the King's Own Scottish Borderers museum in Berwick upon Tweed, although there is a message board for visitors to post enquiries about the regiment's history.

Army And Regimental Museums

Details of all Army and regimental museums can be found at
www.armymuseums.org.uk, which is maintained by the Army Museum
Ogilby Trust. There are details of addresses, opening hours, charges and
locations of archives and, of course, where appropriate there is a link to the
museum's website. You can search by regiment or by location.

www.flying-museum.org.uk offers a comprehensive introduction to the
Museum of Army Flying at Middle Wallop.

www.firepower.org.uk is the website for Firepower – the Royal Artillery
Museum. Despite the cringe making title, it is actually a comprehensive
museum in the old Woolwich Arsenal, where there is an excellent library and
archive.

The Royal Engineers museum website at www.remuseum.org.uk is strangely
set out and organised, but it is informative and attractive, with lots of pages
about the Corps' history, including a short article about how the Sappers
won the FA Cup in 1875. The site works best in Internet Explorer.

www.tankmuseum.co.uk is essentially a site run by enthusiasts for fellow
enthusiasts at the Tank Museum at Bovington, Dorset, but gives a real feel for
what the Museum is about.

www.kingsownbordermuseum.btik.com is an interesting site about the Border Regiment and King's Own Borderers at the Cumbria Military Museum in Carlisle Museum. There are pages with detailed guides to researching men who served with the regiments.

Chester Military Museum, houses the regimental museum and archives of the Cheshire Regiment. The website, at www.chester.ac.uk/militarymuseum, however, could do with updating and expanding.

www.keepmilitarymuseum.org is the site for the regimental museum for the Devonshire and Dorset Regiment at the Keep Museum in Dorchester.

www.durham.gov.uk/dli is the very attractive site for the Durham Light Infantry Museum in Durham, which includes research guides on family history and medals. You can even listen to clips of audio files featuring the reminiscences of old comrades.

The superb website of the Royal Gloucestershire, Berkshire and Wiltshire Regiment at the Wardrobe Museum in the Close at Salisbury can be found at www.thewardrobe.org.uk. It has the best on-line resources of any regimental

museum. In particular, there are sets of war diaries for the Royal Berkshire and Wiltshire regiments for the two world wars available online.

The website of the Soldiers of Gloucestershire Museum at www.glosters.org.uk is very impressive, as well as being useful. There is a database of all the men from the Gloucestershires who served during the First World War, and many of the museum's artefacts have been scanned and images made available through a fully searchable on-line catalogue.

www.greenhowards.org.uk/index.htm takes visitors to the excellent regimental museum in Richmond (North Yorkshire) for the Green Howards, with lots of pages for family historians and people wanting to know more about the regiment and its history. It even explains how to avoid computer viruses!

www.fusiliersmuseum-lancashire.org.uk/index.html links to the attractive website for the Lancashire Fusiliers Museum in Bury, which should move into new premises by the end of 2008.

www.queensroyalsurreys.org.uk tells the story of the two county regiments of Surrey, which are commemorated in rather splendid premises at Clandon House near Guildford, Queen's Royal Surrey. The site has lots of pages devoted to regimental histories and some nice quirky stories.

The site for the Royal Northumberland Fusiliers at www.northumberlandfusiliers.org.uk is rather disappointing but it does contain a catalogue to the archival holdings in the regimental museum at Alnwick Castle.

The Museum of the Soldiers of Oxfordshire Trust, www.sofo.org.uk, is campaigning for a museum to commemorate all the units raised in the county. At present they have indexed their archival holdings (which is available online here) and are looking for a suitable home.

www.wfrmuseum.org.uk links to the website of the regimental museum for the Worcestershire and Sherwood Foresters (29th/45th Foot). There are numerous pages of information, including rolls of honour and profiles of staff members.

Naval Museums

There are two sites that describe naval and maritime museums across the British Isles. The most useful is www.cus.cam.ac.uk/~mhe1000, which offers links to and descriptions of 300 such museums in the United Kingdom and Ireland. More attractive is www.maritimebritain.org.uk, which is a general site for the tourist, although it has links to naval museum websites around

Britain. Unfortunately, many links are broken because it has not been updated recently.

www.fleetairarm.com the Fleet Air Arm Museum is the national museum of naval aviation and is based at Yeovilton in deepest Somerset. The website is a tad disappointing, and can be hard to read, although there are descriptions of the aircraft held in the collection.

The website of the Royal Naval Submarine Museum in Gosport www.rnsubmus.co.uk has many interesting photographs and artefacts, such as a photograph album of the voyage made by HMS *Olympus* in China in 1931. There is also a roll-call of all submarines that have been lost between HMS *A1* in 1904 and HMS *Artemis* in 1971.

www.royalmarinesmuseum.co.uk offers a not terribly informative glimpse into the Royal Marines Museum in Southsea.

www.explosion.org.uk the Museum of Naval Firepower at Gosport has an impressive website (and an unfortunate flash introduction), but not really very much about naval firepower in general.

HMS *Unicorn*, a 46-gun frigate of 1824 is preserved in the Victoria Dock in Dundee and www.frigateunicorn.org is a website devoted to the ship.

Aviation Museums

Both www.aeroflight.co.uk/mus/uk/ukmus-home.htm and www.thunder-and-lightnings.co.uk/links/museums.html have links to many, if not most, aviation museums in the UK. The former is the more comprehensive, as it includes general museums and galleries of interest to air enthusiasts.

And if you want to fly your own plane to these museums, www.greenaway.flyer.co.uk/museums.html tells you how, while www.museum-explorer.org.uk offers details and news of aviation museums across Britain.

www.museumofberkshireaviation.co.uk is the website of the Museum of Berkshire Aviation at Woodley near Reading, once the centre of a thriving aircraft industry. Miles and Handley Page aircraft built there are being reconstructed and exhibited, along with pictorial records and priceless archives.

An unofficial site about the Buntingthorpe Collection of Cold War Aircraft near Lutterworth can be found at http://brunty.bravehost.com. Although interesting it does not give details about how to visit or contact the Collection.

The Helicopter Museum at Weston Super Mare, which has the largest collection of helicopters in the world, is described at www.helicoptermuseum.co.uk.

The Lincolnshire Aviation Museum at East Kirby, which attempts to recreate the atmosphere of a wartime bomber station, has a website at www.lincsaviation.co.uk.

http://rafmillom.co.uk is the website for the RAF Millom Museum in Cumbria. At the time of writing the site is only temporary, but clearly it has been in this state for some months.

www.newarkairmuseum.org the attractive site for the Newark Air Museum in Nottinghamshire, includes a 360-degree view of the main gallery.

The Norfolk and Suffolk Aviation Museum at Flixton, Suffolk has a very informative website about what you will find on a visit (which is free).

The website of the Scottish National Museum of Flight at East Fortune (www.nms.ac.uk/museumofflighthomepage.aspx) has descriptions of many of the aircraft in its collection, as well as pages devoted to the history of flying north of the border.

www.spitfireonline.co.uk takes you to the Solent Spitfire and Hall of Aviation at Southampton. It is a rather disappointing site about a fine museum (with irritating Flash graphics and music you can't turn off), although if you want to hire a replica Spitfire the site will tell you how to go about it.

The Carpet-bagger Aviation Museum at Harrington, Northamptonshire was formed in 1993 to commemorate special operations by the USAAF (Operation CARPETBAGGER) from the airfield, as well those to those of the SOE, which flew out of nearby RAF Tempsford. http://harringtonmuseum.org.uk is the informative website.

There are, of course, hundreds, perhaps thousands, of aviation museums across the world. Here's a small selection of those that caught my attention:

- www.defence.gov.au/RAAF/raafmuseum is the site for the RAAF Museum at Point Cook near Melbourne. There are also several other RAAF museums across South East Australia: www.raafmuseum.com at Townsville, Queensland and www.tourisminternet.com.au/wwraaf.htm at Wagga Wagga, New South Wales.

- One museum I'd like to visit is the Foynes Flying Boat Museum in Ireland found at www.flyingboatmuseum.com, which is where transatlantic flying boats first landed from America during the Second World War. Incidentally, it was here that Irish Coffee was invented to warm and revive chilly passengers.

• www.nationalmuseum.af.mil is for the National Museum of the USAAF, the oldest aviation museum in the world at the Wright-Patterson Air Force Base at Dayton, Ohio.

Chapter 5

THE ARMY

The British Army has been in existence since the early 1660s, although one or two regiments can trace their antecedents back before then. Initially its presence was barely tolerated and each year an Army Act had to be passed so that the Standing Army could continue.

Initially, regiments and corps were formed and disbanded as required, with the regiment taking the name of the colonel who raised it. By the mid-eighteenth century this no longer happened. The first corps of specialist artillery men ('gunners') and engineers ('sappers') were also formed. Regiments also began to be linked to specific counties, which was formalised and encouraged after the Army reforms of the 1880s.

It was not until 1856, following the horrors of the Crimean War, that conditions for ordinary British soldiers began to improve. Before then they were generally badly treated and in return had a justified reputation for drunkenness and bad behaviour. By 1914, however, the ordinary soldier had become a fearsome fighting machine – undoubtedly the best in the world – led by brave but often uninspiring officers. In wartime 'Tommy Atkins' was increasingly eulogised, but unlike his cousin, 'Jack Tar', was generally ignored or distrusted in peacetime.

During the eighteenth and nineteenth centuries the Army fought campaigns on every continent, which are often still commemorated by regiments today. With the exception of the American Revolutionary War, each of these campaigns was ultimately victorious (although it could be argued that the War of 1812 and the Crimean War were 'draws' as there were no clear-cut victors).

Things changed forever on 4 August 1914. Two world wars transformed what was an elite band of volunteers into a Citizen Army of conscripts who had joined only for the 'duration'. Technology, too, became increasingly important as a way of getting an advantage over the enemy, and increasingly as a means of reducing casualties at 'the sharp end'.

In many ways the Army of today is very similar to that of a century ago – overstretched and engaged in short, sharp, colonial-style wars, but still an elite and extremely professional force.

The websites here, and in the sections on the two world wars and the post-war world, offer a fascinating insight into the Army's history.

Background Information

The much respected Society for Army Historical Research encourages research into the history of the British Army. It maintains a functional website at www.edboydenphotos.co.uk/Sahr/sahr.html.

The website of the Scottish Military History Society is at www.btinternet.com/~james.mckay/dispatch.htm and offers information about the society, plus an index to the Society's journal. Members have their own area with many more resources.

Soldier has been the Army's official magazine since the end of the Second World War. As well as stories about today's squaddies, www.soldiermagazine.co.uk has an archive of some 350 articles going back to 1945.

www.britishbattles.com contains accounts of battles from the Hundred Years War to the end of the Boer War, describing the units present and their casualties, and with maps of the field of conflict. Less successful is www.geocities.com/beckster05/index.html, which contains rather text-heavy accounts of a few British battles from Hastings to Trafalgar.

© The Scots at War Trust 2003-06 | Registered Charity No. SC023305

29/1/07

The Home of the Discriminating General at www.militaryheritage.com is an interesting site with much about the British Army between about 1750 and 1850, with pages and related sites concerning the men and the arms they carried.

The excellent www.achart.ca is largely concerned with the schooling of soldiers' children during the nineteenth century. There are also pages on other military historical subjects, as well as copies of correspondence with other researchers.

Slow to load, but extremely useful, is www.rma-searcher.co.uk, which contains lists of boys educated at the Royal Military Asylum at Chelsea and who later enlisted between the 1840s and 1900s. There is even an MP3 file of a broadcast of the old school song.

The website of the Scots at War Trust at www.scotsatwar.org.uk looks at the experiences of Scottish soldiers at home and overseas, with lots of background information.

http://intellit.muskingum.edu/uk_folder/uktoc.html has many pages relating to the British intelligence services and their history. There is a good bibliography. Part of a wider site devoted to intelligence worldwide.

A fascinating and unique site www.psywar.org/leaflets.php provides a history of Psychological Warfare from the First World War to the present day. You will need to register to take full advantage of all the facilities offered.

Uniforms and Equipment

www.militaryfactory.com is an American site devoted to cataloguing military and civilian aircraft, armoured vehicles, individual weapon systems, naval ships and munitions from around the world from the eighteenth century to the present day. There is a search engine to enable you to find your way around the site. A specifically American site is www.olive-drab.com concentrating on US vehicles and equipment, many of which were eventually used by British and Commonwealth forces.

The Gothia Association for Weapons has many pages devoted to Continental, and especially Swedish, small arms at http://gotavapen.se/index_english.htm, and will show you how to field strip a gun – if you really need to know.

The Geometry of War, 1500–1750 at www.mhs.ox.ac.uk/geometry/content.htm has many very detailed pages devoted to early military technology and fortifications considered from a mathematical point of view.

www.radix.net/%7Ebbrown/brit_bayo.html#contents is an extremely comprehensive site devoted to the British bayonet in all its forms.

There are a number of sites for collectors of Mills Grenades, such as www.millsgrenades.co.uk, which is a good place to start. Another site for collectors is www.geocities.com/sf_armourer/armrindex.html. At www.paul-spence1964.com you can even download videos of the webmaster's collection of grenades. Meanwhile, http://members.shaw.ca/dwlynn/tgrm.htm provides a grenade recognition manual to grenades worldwide.

If you are interested in old military vehicles then you should join the Military Vehicle Trust at www.mvt.org.uk. There are pages devoted to the conservation and preservation of former military vehicles, and links to enthusiasts clubs around the world.

The Historic Military Vehicle Forum at www.hmvf.co.uk has a large number of articles on military vehicles worldwide including interviews with collectors.

The Early Military Land Rovers Association at www.emlra.org has pages for people interested in those Land Rovers that saw military service.

www.tankhistory.com is a site devoted to the history of tanks worldwide before 1946, with brief details on individual makes.

www.users.zetnet.co.uk/lsm/dhmg/index.html is very much an enthusiast's site devoted to his obsession for tanks and other heavy military vehicles. There is a lot of interesting material here. And if you want to have a go yourself, www.tankdriving.co.uk will organise a session for you.

There are several museums with collections of military vehicles. The REME Museum at Arborfield near Reading has a large range of kit used by the British Army. More information can be found at www.rememuseum.org.uk. Better known is the Tank Museum at Bovington, www.tankmuseum.co.uk, with a lot for enthusiasts.

Badges

www.militarybadges.org.uk/badges/badgestart.htm is a good place to start to begin identifying Army badges, although it is not really indexed by unit, or by type of badge, so it involves a great deal of scrolling. More fun is www.webshots.com, which consists of uploaded photos submitted by users – particularly useful for regimental badges and uniform badges.

Another collection of mainly modern cap badges can be seen at www.geocities.com/heartland/flats/6804.

www.fovantbadges.com is an interesting site about the Australian and British regimental badges etched into the Wiltshire chalk downs at Fovant Camp during the First World War.

Trooper Bones is a commercial company selling replicas of regimental badges and the equivalents for the RN and RAF at http://trooperbones.com/index.htm. Unfortunately, the design of the homepage is rather bizarre, and links to a number of pages did not work, but at least you can see images of the badges.

Regimental Histories

As well as sites listed below, it is worth checking the list of regimental museums in Chapter 4, which often contain useful material.

One of the most important military history websites (it's in my top ten, see p. 202) is Land Forces of the British Empire at http://regiments.org. It was launched back in 1995 to provide details of every regiment and corps in the British and Commonwealth armies. From the Adjutant-General's Department to the Yorkshire Volunteers via the Camel Corps and the Glider Pilot Regiment. The intention was that for each unit there would be details of title and lineage, when it was formed and disbanded, where it served and battle honours, colonels and links to museums and other websites of interest. To a large extent the aims have been met, although the site does remain incomplete. Unfortunately, it is no longer being updated – the last one seems to have taken place in July 2004 – which is a great shame. Even so it remains an excellent resource.

The Army pages on the MOD website have pages about current units and their history at www.army.mod.uk.

www.qaranc.co.uk is an excellent site about the history of Queen Alexandra's Army Nursing Corps (nicknamed 'the Grey Mafia') and the former Army Nursing Service.

There are many sites about units in the Royal Artillery, which are mainly for old comrades. These also include a little history: www.22oca.org.uk – 22 Regiment; www.36regimentra.org.uk – 36 Heavy Air Defence Regiment; www.oca42regt.com/homepage.htm – 42 Regiment RA Old Comrades, and www.duffy-eu.com/94loc/index.htm – 94 Locating Regiment (and includes material about other survey regiments).

http://hometown.aol.com/reubique has many pages about the history of the Royal Engineers. Unfortunately, it is extremely slow to load, even with broadband, which makes it almost impossible to use.

An interesting site about the Royal Engineers in British Columbia in the 1850s and 1860s, maintained by a re-enactment group, is at www.royalengineers.ca. Photographs taken by the Royal Engineers while stationed at Halifax, Nova Scotia during the 1870s and 1880s are at www.gov.ns.ca/nsarm/cap/royalengineers.

www.rlc-conductor.info has pages about the history of the Conductor, which is a senior warrant officer position, in the Royal Logistics Corps and its predecessors. The website argues that it has been in existence for 600 years. Some interesting material on an unusual topic.

http://royalpioneercorps.co.uk/rpc/history.htm tells the history of the Royal Pioneer Corps and its predecessors, with well-laid out pages on researching ancestors who were members of the Corps and an illustrated history.

The founder of the Boy Scouts, Robert Baden-Powell spent most of his military career with the 13th Hussars.

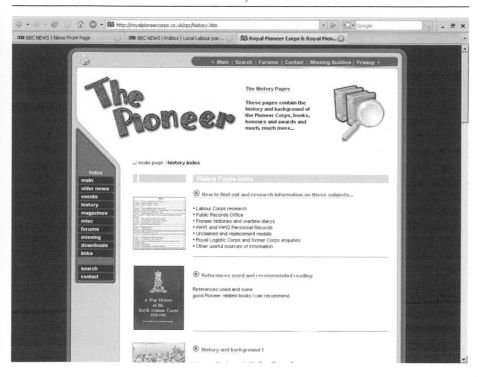

http://pinetreeweb.com/bp-hussars.htm explores his career and is quite informative about this cavalry regiment in the late Victorian period.

The website of a current cavalry regiment, the 1st Queen's Dragoon Guards – www.qdg.org.uk – has a mixture of information about the regiment and history. Of particularly interest are a selection of veterans' diaries? held by the regimental archives and pages about the uniforms worn over the centuries.

Although disbanded more than thirty years ago, the 10th Royal Hussars (Prince of Wales Own) has not been forgotten. www.10thhussar.com is a mixture of regimental history and meeting place for former regimental members. Another website about the regiment is at www.xrhgb.com.

The Honourable Artillery Company is the oldest unit in the British Army, founded in 1537. However, www.hac.org.uk is mainly about the HAC today.

http://web.ukonline.co.uk/ewh.bryan/Cheshire-1.htm has a lot of information about the Cheshire Regiment (22nd Foot). Also worth visiting is www.cheshireregiment.org.uk. Meanwhile, http://h-joswick.tripod.com/22ndregiment/index.html is an American re-enactment group recreating the regiment as it was during the late 1770s.

www.devils-own.co.uk is a site for an Anglo-Irish band of re-enactors recreating the 88th Foot (Connaught Rangers) in the Napoleonic Wars. There are some pages about the regiment's history and a strip cartoon drawn by one of the members about life as a re-enactor.

http://royaldublinfusiliers.com is a new site about the history of the Royal Dublin Fusiliers between its formation in 1881 and disbandment in 1922.

www.lancs-fusiliers.co.uk is the old comrades association for the XXth Lancashire Fusiliers, with lots of pages devoted to former soldiers in the regiment.

An on-line exhibition about the Oxfordshire Yeomanry is at www.oxfordshire.gov.uk/wps/portal/publicsite/councilservices?WCM_GL OBAL_CONTEXT=http://apps.oxfordshire.gov.uk/wps/wcm/connect/Int ernet/Council+services/Leisure+and+culture/Museums/Online+exhibition s/Oxfordshire+Yeomanry. This wins the award for the longest URL in the book, but there is no other way of getting to what is a very interesting website.

The regimental association for the Queen's Own Buffs (Princess of Wales Royal Regiment) at www.the-queens-own-buffs.com has pages about the Second World War and the Malayan Emergency. See also www.2nd-queens.com, for the Second Battalion.

The Somerset Military Museum in Taunton at www.sommilmuseum.org.uk has material about the Somerset Light Infantry and other units raised in the county.

www.btinternet.com/~the35thfootproject/index.html is the website of a re-enactment group for the 35th Foot (Royal Sussex Regiment) mainly recreating the period of the Seven Years War. There are pages of regimental history and related tourist sites of interest. The Royal Sussex Living History Group concentrates on the late Victorian and Edwardian period and is at www.royalsussex.org.uk. The website contains pages on the history of the regiment.

A collection of artefacts for the Royal Welch Fusiliers found in Welsh museums is at http://www.gtj.org.uk/en/subjects/3647.

www.worcestershireregiment.com is a very attractive and useful virtual museum for the Worcestershire Regiment, with lots of resources and information. Unfortunately the site was down at the time of writing.

www.19thfoot.co.uk – is a re-enactment group for the 19th Foot (Green Howards), which specialise in the Crimean War. There are also pages on the history of the regiment. A page about the career of Patrick McNamara, who joined the 19th Foot in 1847 is at http://members.ozemail.com.au/~clday/19foot.htm.

http://website.lineone.net/~bwir tells the story of the regiments raised in the British West Indies from the late eighteenth century until the 1960s.

The history of the First Air Nursing Yeomanry (FANY), which supplied volunteer women drivers etc. in the First World War and wireless operators in the Second world War (including a few who were dropped into occupied France), and is still active in its centenary year, is told at www.fany.org.uk.

Chapter 6

THE ROYAL NAVY
1700–1919

U ntil well into the twentieth century the Royal Navy was the main defence of the British Isles, and even when the Army was neglected (as it often was), ships were built and new technologies developed and introduced. An excellent introduction to the history of the 'Senior Service' is provided by the Ministry of Defence at www.royal-navy.mod.uk/server/show/nav.3839.

Naval And Maritime History

The following sites contain pages or provide contacts for the study of naval history in its widest form, although they all have material about the Royal Navy:

- The Society for Nautical Research, Britain's premier naval research society founded in 1910 has a website at www.snr.org.uk describing the Society's activities. It publishes the much-respected *Mariner's Mirror*.

- Less academic is Naval Historical Collectors and Research Association. Its website www.nhcra-online.org/main.htm has a few articles about ships and the men who served on them.

- As the name suggests, the Naval Dockyard Society exists to encourage research in naval dockyards. More can be found at www.hants.gov.uk/navaldockyard.

- www.hnsa.org/index.htm provides a guide to historic Navy ships worldwide, including eight in Britain, which are open to the public.

- www.cus.cam.ac.uk/~mhe1000 had lists of 300 naval museums across the British Isles with links to many of them.

National Historic Ships is a quango advising the government about historic ships. It maintains the National Register of Historic Vessels, containing information about some 1,200 surviving ships in the United Kingdom. More about its work can be found at www.nhsc.org.uk.

www.shotguncharlie.co.uk/nauticalclub.htm is the website of London's Nautical Club, but mostly of interest because it contains links to lots of old comrade associations.

www.deepimage.co.uk/homepages/mainsitepages/shipwreckshome.html is a fascinating site devoted to deep-sea diving, with some interesting pages and photographs relating to Royal Navy wrecks.

www.thamestugs.com is devoted to tugs that worked on the Thames, a few of which ended in naval service.

www.rootsweb.com/~bmuwgw/ships.html contains brief histories of ships, naval and merchant, which arrived at Bermuda from the sixteenth century onwards.

One of the strangest English-language websites must be the history of Turkish submarines at www.geocities.com/Pentagon/Bunker/7704/index.html. Yet this is a detailed and impressive site. The same webmaster also has a site about the modern Turkish Navy at www.turkishnavy.nct.

Largely a naval war, the Russo-Japanese War (1904–1905) must have been one of weirdest and one-sided of modern times. Find out more at www.russojapanesewar.com.

http://vlnavmar.usnaweb.org/index_long.html has hundreds of links to (mostly American) websites concerned with naval history, although many are broken.

Background Information

www.swmaritime.org.uk/article.php?articleid=553&atype=a has details about the publicity-shy Naval Historical Branch, a body seemingly without any other presence on the web. However, the contacts should be treated with caution, as they may well be out of date.

Navy News has been reporting on the Royal Navy since the 1940s. Its comprehensive website, www.navynews.co.uk, is mainly about today's Navy, but there are some pages on the service's history.

www.cronab.demon.co.uk offers a superb resource about the Royal Navy between the eighteenth and twentieth centuries, although it is pot luck whether you will find what you are looking for. Even if you don't, you are likely to be diverted to something more interesting. Unfortunately, it is hard to navigate (you need to keep scrolling down the home page) and is very text-heavy.

www.bruzelius.info/Nautica/Naval_History/GB/TOC.html contains many pages about the early history of the Royal Navy. They are generally extracts from contemporary letters and documents between 1546 and 1817.

A rather irritating site is www.cyber-heritage.co.uk, partly because of its jokey style and poor design (not for nothing does the webmaster Steve Johnson call his site 'content over style'), but there is a lot of good material here, mainly about the Navy in the late nineteenth and twentieth centuries.

Royal Navy Ships

www.cronab.demon.co.uk/INTRO.HTM lists all sailing ships that served with the Royal Navy plus a brief history of each. The website also has an excellent introduction to Navy sailing ships, and how they were run can be found at www.cronab.demon.co.uk/gen1.htm.

www.nelsonsnavy.freesurf.fr is a list of ships appearing in Steel's Navy List of April 1794. For each ship there are brief details of the number of guns and her station. Somehow one feels that there should be a lot more.

www.battleships-cruisers.co.uk/royal.htm is database of RN ships after 1860, with photographs you can buy, and brief details about the ship, as well as contributions from visitors to the site. You will need to scroll down the page to find what you want. The main site offers the same facility for most other navies of the world.

www.geocities.com/Pentagon/Quarters/7155/ contains photos of the Victorian Navy (also links to other sites mainly relating to the RN in Portsmouth). It is part of a much wider site, www.cyber-heritage.co.uk, although there is no obvious link between the two.

Much more useful is www.navyphotos.co.uk, which contains a collection of naval photos from the mid-nineteenth century until the millennium.

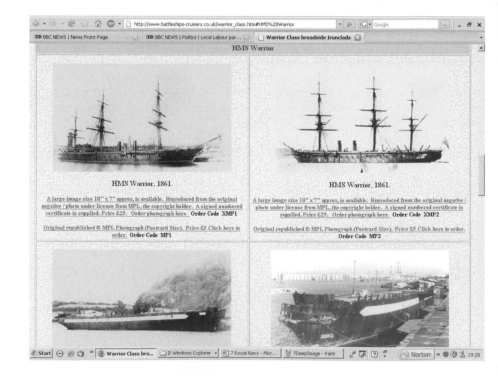

More modern photographs of ships in the twentieth century for the Royal Navy (and other navies worldwide) can be found at www.maritimequest.com/index.htm

www.dreadnoughtproject.org is devoted to 3D models of dreadnoughts and other pre-First World War battleships from Britain, Germany and Austria-Hungary. There are some excellent images and models.

www.bobhenneman.info is an American site devoted to pre-First World War battlecruisers (including those of the Royal Navy), including descriptions of each one both built and projected. The most interesting pages are about the salvage of these vessels and include some nice pictures.

www.tallshipbounty.org is about the replica HMS *Bounty*, which was built in 1960 for the film *Mutiny on the Bounty* (as well as material on the original ship). It is possible to book passage on the ship if you want to experience life on board. If you are interested in the mutiny itself, www.lareau.org/bounty.html offers a comprehensive introduction, including an exhaustive debate on the causes.

The campaign to save HMS *Cerebus*, the first steam monitor built for the Royal Navy and now rotting near Melbourne, can be found at www.cerberus.com.au.

www.anmm.gov.au/site/page.cfm?u=457 is an interesting site about Captain Cook's ship HMS *Endeavour* and the replica at the Australian National Maritime Museum in Sydney.

www.hmsgangesassoc.org – site for sailors who were trained at HMS *Ganges*, with pages about the history of the training establishment and photographs.

The restored frigate HMS *Trincomalee*, originally built in Bombay in 1816–1817, is now at Hartlepool. The website www.hms-trincomalee.co.uk has lots about its history, plus interactive tours etc.

www.hms-victory.com is the official HMS *Victory* website, with an interactive tour of the ship plus a crew list for the Battle of Trafalgar. More about HMS *Victory*, as well as the Battle of St Vincent, can be found at www.stvincent.ac.uk/Heritage/1797/index2.html.

A modern project to build a cutter as they would have done two centuries ago is detailed at http://www.hamstat.demon.co.uk/Victory/index_v.htm. You will need to scroll down the home page to get to the relevant pages.

www.weymouthdiving.co.uk/book_intr.htm looks at the loss of the East Indiaman *Earl of Abergavenny* off Weymouth in 1805. William Wordsworth's brother, John, was the captain.

More about individual ships of the later periods can be found in the sections devoted to the two world wars and the post-war Navy.

The Eighteenth Century And Napoleonic Wars

For obvious reasons, the Royal Navy of the late eighteenth century and early nineteenth centuries has always fascinated historians and researchers. This has a led to a large number of websites, although many were created to coincide with the bicentenary of the Battle of Trafalgar in 2005:

www.users.bigpond.com/ShipStreetPress/Snell/Index.htm tells the story of Hannah Snell, who spent two years disguised as a man in the Royal Marines in the 1740s. Also included are the stories of several other women who enlisted in the services as men.

Senior Service is a re-enactment group specialising in the Navy of the 1740s. Find out more at http://homepage.ntlworld.com/gc.hughes/senserv.htm.

www.captaincooksociety.com is the website of the Captain Cook Society, with information about the great explorer, including extracts from his journals.

www.hmsrichmond.org is an American re-enactment site devoted to recreating life on-board HMS *Richmond*, a frigate during the American Revolutionary Wars. There's an interesting page explaining the historical terms in use in about 1775.

A most unusual resource is the diary of Aaron Thomas, a seaman on-board HMS *Lapwing* in the Caribbean in 1798 and 1799. It has been transcribed and is now available online at http://scholar.library.miami.edu/thomas.

An interesting website with background information on life in the Navy between the 1790s and 1810s is 'Broadside', which can be found at www.nelsonsnavy.co.uk. Another useful essay on life below decks at the period is at www.channel4.com/history/microsites/H/history/n-s/nelson.html.

Lesley and Roy Adkins have written several books about Nelson's Navy and circulate what they call 'The Occasional Newsletter', which is sent out to subscribers three or four times a year. It covers aspects of early nineteenth-century naval history, interesting memorials they have come across and much else. It is well worth subscribing to. Details at www.adkinsarchaeology.com.

Yet another introductory site to Nelson's Navy is http://home.gci.net/~stal, although it is by no means complete.

The Historical Maritime Society (which despite the grand name is a group of re-enactors specialising in the period) has a page of FAQs relating to the period at www.hms.org.uk, which should answer many questions. They also have pages of extensive links to many other naval sites.

There are several sites devoted to the life of Admiral Lord Nelson, including www.aboutnelson.co.uk and www.admiralnelson.org., which is an attractive life of Nelson as if written by the great man himself. As a masterful self-publicist all too aware of spin, Nelson would surely have had his own blog had he been alive today!

The Nelson Society, www.nelson-society.org.uk, exists to commemorate the great man's life and contains a number of interesting pages.

There is an excellent on-line exhibition on Nelson from the National Maritime Museum at www.nmm.ac.uk/server/show/ConWebDoc.21155. As well as pages relating to the biography of Nelson there is also introductory material relating to the Navy of the period.

A selection of Nelson's despatches and letters are available at www.wtj.com/archives/nelson.

A page of links to other sites about Nelson is at www.geocities.com/Athens/3682/lord_nelson.html. Unfortunately, some are likely to be broken because they have not been updated since 2001.

The official site commemorating the 200th Anniversary of the Battle of Trafalgar is at www.paintedships.com, although no longer maintained it still has some interesting pages. An animation of the battle showing how it took place is at www.bbc.co.uk/history/british/empire_seapower/launch_ani_trafalgar.sht ml. The BBC site also has pages discussing the battle, its impact and life on-board ships of the period.

There are a number of accounts of the battle: a reliable, if rather text-heavy one, can be found at www.geocities.com/beckster05/index.html.

Admiral Collinwood's despatch announcing the great victory and Nelson's death, which arrived in London a fortnight after the battle, can be found at www.bruzelius.info/Nautica/Naval_History/GB/Times(1805–11–07)a.html

For more affluent readers, Sim Comfort Associates offer high-quality reproductions of books about naval warfare between 1793 and 1815. More details at www.simcomfort.demon.co.uk.

HMS *Surprise*, http://home.wxs.nl/~pdavis/index.htm, was originally a site about William Loney (1817–1898), a nineteenth-century naval surgeon, but has developed into a superb resource about the late eighteenth- and early nineteenth-century Navy. You can even download software allowing you to 'navigate' a Navy frigate of the period – fascinating.

The Nineteenth And Twentieth Centuries

www.btinternet.com/~philipr/content.htm is an excellent site on the Victorian and Edwardian Royal Navy, which is curiously a rather neglected subject online. There are also many pages on late nineteenth century around the world.

http://hmsbelfast.iwm.org.uk is the IWM microsite for HMS *Belfast*, which served at D-Day and then after the war. It includes some useful on-line exhibitions about the Royal Navy in the twentieth century.

www.pbenyon.plus.com/Seamanship_Man/Details_Org_Alpha.html displays extracts from the Manual of Seamanship for 1932, offering a fascinating insight into the organisation of naval ships of the 1930s.

An interesting site is www.hmsfalcon.com, which is about the Royal Navy river gunboats that patrolled China from the end of the nineteenth century until after the Second World War. Unfortunately, the text is reversed out blue on black, so it can be difficult to read.

www.yalumba.co.uk/Framesets/British%20Power%20Boat%20Co.htm tells the story of the British Power Boats Co., which built many motor torpedo boats for the RN and RAF before and during the Second World War.

First World War

Although the Royal Navy was the most powerful in the world and millions of pounds had been spent on creating a modern fleet, it could be argued that it did not have a good war. The only battle of consequence was the Battle of Jutland at the end of May 1916, which many observers consider a draw, although it had the effect of keeping the German High Seas Fleet bottled up until the end of the war. The Navy was also slow to work out how to protect convoys bringing vital supplies from North America.

Meanwhile, online, there are two excellent introductions to the war at sea, which should be your first port of call:

www.worldwar1.co.uk, which is perhaps more for beginners and has brief descriptions of British and some German ships.

www.worldwar1atsea.net, more for the advanced researcher and has material about all the navies of the period. Its sister site www.naval-history.net also has relevant pages, although it is largely for the Second World War.

A list and descriptions of RN ships taken from *Jane's Fighting Ships* for 1919 can be found at www.pbenyon1.plus.com/Janes_1919/Index.html.

www.hmshampshire.co.uk is about the sinking of HMS *Hampshire* in June 1916 with the loss of 643 lives, including that of the Secretary of State for, War Lord Kitchener. His death was perhaps a blessing in disguise, as Kitchener was increasingly seen by politicians as being an unsuitable leader in a world of total warfare. The sinking led to a number of inter-war conspiracy theories.

www.mckenzie.uk.com/zeebrugge/index.htm tells the story of Able Seaman Albert McKenzie of HMS *Vindictive*, who won the VC during the Raid on Zeebrugge in April 1918.

The diaries of Petty Officer George William Smith DSM, of HMS *Borodino*, covering the North Russian Expedition of 1918–1919, may be found at www.naval-history.net/WW1z05NorthRussia.htm.

Not all naval men served at sea, some 50,000 were sent to fight in the Royal Naval Divisions in France. www.royalnavaldivision.co.uk/index.htm tells the story of a few of them. You can download Divisional diaries and service records for the men at www.nationalarchives.gov.uk/documentsonline.

www.jackclegg.com is the story of Marine Jack Clegg, who served in the Royal Marines Light Infantry, and his fellow marines from Barnsley. There are also more general pages about the Royal Marines and the Royal Naval Division.

Chapter 7

AVIATION AND THE ROYAL AIR FORCE – GENERAL WEBSITES AND FIRST WORLD WAR

Manned flight did not come until as late as December 1901, and it was a few years until pilots began to take to the air in Britain. Over the past century aviation – and military aviation in particular – has rapidly progressed in speed, endurance and ability, in order to deliver what commanders in the field demand of the air arm.

In this chapter, we look at general websites for the history of aviation (both British and overseas) and the RAF, and also consider sites covering the early days of military flight until the formation of the RAF in April 1918.

British Aviation

www.air-britain.com/index.html is the home of Air Britain, which claims to be 'The world's leading organisation for aviation enthusiasts' – mainly a publisher, but it has a useful database of aircraft photographs. www.flypast.com is the website of *Fly Past* magazine and has a useful glossary of terms used in aviation.

The British Aircraft Directory www.britishaircraft.co.uk/aircraft.html contains drawings of all aircraft flown by the RAF and its predecessors (or built in Britain) with technical specifications.

Details of all airfields in the UK between 1909 and 1944 can be found at www.homepages.mcb.net/bones/06airfields/UK/uk.htm.

The history of aviation in the North East of England mainly in the 1930s and early 1940s is discussed at http://norav.50megs.com.

www.colinfparsons.btinternet.co.uk/twinp/colhome/eastchurch/ default.htm contains an article about memorials to early aviation pioneers on the Isle of Sheppey.

www.diverse-images.com is a Brighton company that makes top-quality models for collectors and enthusiasts. They are a world away from the Frog Plastic aeroplane models that were made from 1966. Their fascinating history is told at www.frogpenguin.com.

http://airminded.org is a blog mainly considering air power and British society 1908–1941.

Air Forces Worldwide

An attractive American website devoted to many aspects of aviation history is at www.historicwings.com/index.html. You can download free desktop wallpaper of your favourite aircraft.

Another American site offering a general history is at www.century-of-flight.net/index.htm. There are many pages, for example on the development of jets and flying boats.

http://avia.russian.ee/index2.html is an Estonian site with brief descriptions and specifications of most aircraft types built worldwide, including experimental models. Another site along similar lines is www.altgame.net/aircraft/airstart.html, which is slightly better designed.

The impressive www.aeroflight.co.uk has histories of the world's air forces, the aircraft they fly and details of aviation museums across the globe.

http://users.accesscomm.ca/magnusfamily/airaces1.htm is devoted to air aces – generally pilots who have shot down five or more enemy aircraft. Another site along the same lines is a Czech site at http://aces.safarikovi.org.

Brief histories of all RAAF squadrons and a few other establishments can be found at www.defence.gov.au/RAAF/raafmuseum/research/units.htm.

A history of the Belgian Air Force and military flying in Belgium is maintained by the Belgian Aviation History Association at www.baha.be.

www.rcaf.com is a handsome and detailed site dedicated to the history of the Royal Canadian Air Force. www.jfchalifoux.com is a slightly strange site about the RCAF (and other Canadian military formations) based on the badges collected by its webmaster. Unlike many similar sites, the badges are scanned at a high enough resolution to make them easily readable.

http://home.mit.bme.hu/~tade/history-af.html contains a history of the Hungarian Air Force, plus a variety of other aviation subjects of interest to the webmaster.

The history of the Imperial Iranian Air Force is told at www.iiaf.net/home.html. Clearly the webmaster has a longing for the period before the revolution of 1979.

www.saairforce.co.za is an unofficial site about the South African Air Force, mostly voicing current concerns, but there are a few pages covering its history. If you get bored there are even a couple of games, although they are slow to download.

A handsomely presented history of flying in Sweden, with details of aircraft and military units, can be found at www.canit.se/~griffon/aviation.

http://home.att.net/~jbaugher/usafserials.html provides all you ever needed to know about the issuing of serial numbers to aircraft in the USAAF and USAF since 1921. A database of serial numbers is at http://users.rcn.com/jeremy.k/serialSearch.html.

A database of USAAF/USAF accident reports, including crashes in Britain and Ireland, is at www.accident-report.com/usaf.html. It is possible to buy copies of the reports themselves online.

The history of the Yugoslav Air Force is told at www.yumodel.co.yu. Despite the bizarre layout there is a lot of interesting material.

http://fly.to/AirNet offers 25,000 links to aviation sites around the world. You have to scroll down to find the categories, which are arranged simply. Inevitably, of course, a proportion of links are broken.

Royal Air Force

The best place to start is by looking at the pages about RAF history on the official RAF website, www.raf.mod.uk/history. Unfortunately, at the time of writing, it was being redesigned and improved, although some material is still available at www.raf.mod.uk/history_old/rafhis.html – including a guide to researching RAF history and details of the RAF Historical Society.

www.raf.mod.uk/history/histories.html contains brief histories of RAF units. Again, at the time of writing, it was not functioning, presumably because it is part of the wider redesign of the RAF's own history pages.

www.griffon.clara.net/rafh/heraldry.htm is the infuriating website of the RAF Heraldry Trust. Infuriating because you can't click on the badges to see them enlarged and there is no explanatory text on individual badges and how they came to be chosen by squadrons and units.

www.associations.rafinfo.org.uk has lots of valuable information about the RAF and researching its history, but mainly comprises links to veterans associations in the RAF and sister air forces. To enter you have to click on the RAF flag at the top left of the homepage.

Members of the Women's Auxiliary Air Force (WAAF) played an important role as clerks, radar operators, cooks and mechanics, www.waafassociation.org.uk tells their story.

Aviation Archaeology

For some reason air crash investigation and archaeology groups often have very interesting websites, which include some of the case studies of digs they have undertaken:

www.aviationarchaeology.com is an excellent American site covering the recovery of crashed aircraft worldwide, including some British material. Similar is www.tighar.org, published by the International Group for Historic Aircraft Recovery, although they concentrate on the techniques of recovery rather than the digs themselves.

Ministry of Defence advice about finding and excavating aircraft can be found at www.mod.uk/DefenceInternet/AboutDefence/WhatWeDo/Personnel/AFPAA/AviationArchaeology.htm.

www.gpswalker.cwc.net describes where the remains of RAF crashes can be seen – usually in the upland areas. A lot of pages don't open, however, and the design leaves a lot to be desired.

The Air Crash Investigation and Archaeology Group covers Southern Scotland and Northern England with a website at www.acia.co.uk.

The Borders Historical Aviation Archaeology at www.ezraysnet.co.uk/bhaa/index.html has details of some of the crashes they have investigated in North Wales and the Marches.

The East Anglian Aircraft Research Group investigates air crashes in Eastern England with examples of case studies devoted to some of their investigations at www.sweffling.freeserve.co.uk.

http://web.ukonline.co.uk/lait/site/index.htm is the excellent and informative website for the Lancashire Air Investigation Team. The pages relating to their co-operation with a *Team Time* TV programme are particularly worth reading.

The Manx Aviation Preservation Society, which runs the small Manx Aviation and Military Museum at Douglas Airport has pages about crashes (and the museum) at www.maps.iofm.net.

www.peakdistrictaircrashes.co.uk looks at aircraft crashes in and around the Peak District.

www.scotcrash.homecall.co.uk is the wonderfully self-deprecating site of 'Two men and a dog boldly go to seek out historic aircraft crash sites among the Hills, Munros and Mountains of Scotland' with some nice photographs.

www.aviationmuseum.co.uk is the website of the Thames Aviation Museum at the Coalhouse Fort in Tilbury with pages about the digs undertaken by museum staff and volunteers.

Although difficult to read, www.allenby.info is a fine site, exploring aircraft crashes in and around the North Yorkshire Moors.

A French aviation archaeology group investigating crashes in south-east France and Piedmont has a website at www.aero-relic.org/English/Presentation/e-01-presentation.htm.

First World War

In 1914 military aviation was in its infancy On the outbreak of war the four squadrons of the Royal Flying Corps, totalling 105 officers, 63 aeroplanes, and 95 lorries were sent to France. Left at home were 116 aircraft (described as 'mainly junk'), 41 officers and a few hundred airmen. By the armistice of 1918 the Royal Air Force had 188 squadrons spread across the world engaged in reconnaissance, air defence and even bombing enemy targets, with 22,467 aircraft and 103 airships on strength, and 27,000 officers and 264,000 other ranks including 25,000 women.

www.theaerodrome.com/index.html is general site about First World War aviation, featuring a number of pages for British air forces. Another site, American this time, is www.wwiaviation.com, which offers similar information.

The Rosebud WW1 and Early Aviation Image Archive is a fascinating site at www.earlyaviator.com, looking at European and American aviation photographs, postcards and other images from the earliest days of flying up to 1920.

www.crossandcockade.com is the home page of the Cross and Cockcade Society, which is devoted to First World War Aviation History.

www.cbrnp.com/profiles/quarter1/index.html has drawings of First World War aircraft, largely for modellers, but with additional information as well. Unfortunately, the site has not been updated since 2002. There are also pages on selected aircraft for other periods up to the present day. Another site for modellers is at www.wwi-models.org, which concentrates largely on the First World War period.

The British Anzani Company was founded in 1912 to make engines for aircraft, and after the First World War for motorcycles. www.britishanzani.co.uk tells its story and offers help if you own one of its engines.

www.avro504.org has a lot about the Avro 504 fighter plane, including plans to build a replica. Unfortunately, the use of Flash and poor navigation leaves a lot to be desired.

www.patrickwilson.com/RFC.html tells the story of 100 Squadron RFC/RAF with photographs and an interview with last surviving member. A not dissimilar site for 66 Squadron is at www.66squadron.co.uk.

http://home.btclick.com/rcoleman/narbaero/aerohistory01.htm has pages on the history of Narborough airfield in West Norfolk between 1915 and 1919. The site works best in Internet Explorer.

Albert Ball VC was the greatest British air ace of the war. His story is told at www.albertball.homestead.com. Billy Bishop VC was the greatest Empire air ace and some polemical pages about his career can be found at www.billybishop.net.

Almost forgotten, except to his immediate family, is Lt George R Craig MC, 44 Squadron, who died in an air accident at Hainault in August 1917. More about him can be found at www.prcraig.com.

The Icelandic-Canadian Konnie Johannesson served as a flying instructor in Egypt. A number of the photographs he took while in the RFC/RAF and later are at www.kw.igs.net/~brianj.

The scrapbook and other papers of an American who flew with the RFC, Wendell Phillipo Loomis, has been digitised at www.ww1aviator.com.

Chapter 8

WARS AND CAMPAIGNS 1066–1914

Medieval And Tudor Warfare

A rather text-heavy introduction to the Battle of Hastings can be found at www.geocities.com/beckster05/Hastings/HaPrelude.html. More attractive introductions are at www.battle-of-hastings-1066.org.uk and http://members.tripod.com/~Battle_of_Hastings. An account of the battle

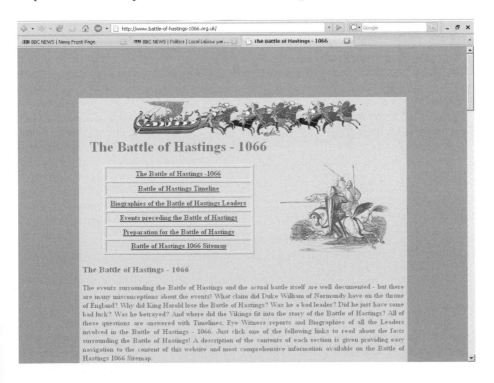

by the chronicler William of Malmesbury is at www.fordham.edu/
halsall/source/1066malmesbury.html.

There are several sites on the Battle of Hastings for schools, including
www.battle1066.com, which provides the background. A fun game allowing
you to be William or Harold is at http://www.bbc.co.uk/history/british/
normans/launch_gms_battle_hastings.shtml.

A general site about medieval castles is at www.camelotintl.com/heritage/
castles/index.html. More information about Welsh castles can be found at
http://www.castlewales.com/home.html.

www.heartofsuffolk.com/FINTROfinal.html – a tourist site but with pages
about medieval moats (and Second World War airfields) showing where they
are to be found today.

The English conquest of Ireland is described by the chronicler Gerald of
Wales at www.fordham.edu/halsall/source/12Cgerald-ireland2.html.

The Battle of Agincourt is discussed at
www.geocities.com/beckster05/Agincourt/AgCampaign.html and
www.aginc.net/battle. Names of 1,200 of the 5,700 men on the English side
can be found at www.familychronicle.com/agincort.htm.

English Civil War

A simple introduction to the War can be found at
http://easyweb.easynet.co.uk/~crossby/ECW. More comprehensive,
however, are pages at www.british-civil-wars.co.uk/index.htm and
www.historyofwar.org/articles/wars_ecw1.html.

Material about the Civil War in Lincolnshire is at
www.rjplincs.plus.com/ariwxe1CivilWar(home.htm and a summary of the
events in neighbouring Nottinghamshire at
www.nottshistory.org.uk/events.htm.

www.eventplan.co.uk/Articles.htm contains an interesting series of articles,
mainly on Civil War, such as on the use of drums by both sides and the Siege
of Bolingbroke Castle in 1643.

A useful chronology to the main events during the English Civil War is at
www.theteacher99.btinternet.co.uk/ecivil/index.htm.

Pages about the life of Oliver Cromwell, the Lord Protector, can be found at
www.lib.cam.ac.uk/Exhibitions/Cromwell/index.htm.

The English Civil War Society at http://english-civil-war-society.org represents re-enactor groups of both Cavaliers and the Roundheads. As well as pages on the groups and where they may be seen, there are also a few pages on the armies and the battles they fought. When I was a student, a number of my fellow students were members of the Sealed Knot. After all these years I was pleased to find that they are still going and maintain an informative website: www.thesealedknot.org.uk.

Eighteenth Century Wars

Pulteney's Regiment (13th Foot) is a living history group, which specialises in the mid-eighteenth century. Their website at http://freespace.virgin.net/gerald.hughes had a history of the unit and demonstrations of drill used during the period. A related body is the mounted Cobham's (10th Dragoons). http://homepage.ntlworld.wm/jc.hughes/cobham/index.htm?cobintw.hml content.

http://members.tripod.com/hm10thregtmusic is the website for the musicians of 10th Regiment of Foot (an American organisation). Sadly it is very out date, but there is a lot of interest here.

www.militaryheritage.com/7yrswar.htm has many pages about the Seven Years War (1756–1763) with pages on uniforms, biographies of officers and eyewitness accounts. There are also sound clips of the kind of music played at the time.

There is a database of members of Royal Lancashire Volunteers from 1779 to the 1790s at www.gmcro.co.uk/sources/mindex.htm.
Inevitably, most of the sites devoted to the War of Independence are American, containing varying levels of patriotic fervour. It is difficult to find websites that are either neutral or from the British perspective, but here is a selection:

Britain's pre-eminent military historian, Richard Holmes, has provided an introductory essay at www.bbc.co.uk/history/british/empire_seapower/rebels_redcoats_01.shtml. A more comprehensive account is at www.historyofwar.org/articles/wars_american_independence.

The US Military Academy at www.dean.usma.edu/history/web03/atlases/american%20revolution has many maps of campaigns and battles, also facsimiles of contemporary mapping. Another site with contemporary maps of North America is http://memory.loc.gov/ammem/gmdhtml/ www.rjplincs.plus.com/ariwxe1CivilWar(home.htm armhtml/armhome.html.

www.si.umich.edu/spies contains facsimiles and transcripts of letters from spies and espionage related activities, both for the rebels and the British.

www.revwar75.com contains extracts from the orderly books, which are roughly equivalent to orders of battles for both sides.

www.royalprovincial.com/index.htm has many pages about the Loyalists (that is, those people who remained loyal to the Crown), whose history is often forgotten. Unfortunately, the site was not working in May 2007.

Biographies of a few British soldiers in the American Revolutionary War can be found at www.silverwhistle.co.uk.

http://home.earthlink.net/~colscoy is an interesting website for the Californian 33rd Regiment of Foot re-enactment group, with some useful background about the conditions endured by soldiers. Butler's Rangers are another such group – http://iaw.on.ca/~awoolley/brang/brang.html – this time representing a regiment recruited from loyalists in New York and Pennsylvania.

Napoleonic Wars

The French Revolutionary and Napoleonic Wars raged between 1793 and 1815, punctuated by a few months of peace in 1802. Some historians have argued that it was the first 'world war' because campaigns were fought in the Americas, India, Egypt, as well as across Europe. The initial intention was to destroy the 'bacillus' of democracy and reason created by the French Revolution, but it soon became a war to contain French attempts to dominate Europe and in particular one man Napoleon Bonaparte, undoubtedly the greatest Frenchman of all time.

A primer on the wars and their effect on life in Regency Britain, including a few short regimental histories and pages on the lives of the soldiery, is at http://homepages.ihug.co.nz/~awoodley/Regency.html. A list of members of the Napoleonic Wars webring can be found at http://pub48.bravenet.com/sitering/show.php?usernum=4053317280, which provides a wide range of interesting websites to visit.

An excellent site providing background information about the armies of all sides is www.napoleonguide.com/armyind.htm. There are many interesting pages about the British Army, including statistics about casualties and a list of medical men killed in the Peninsula. You can also download maps of the key battles or buy reproductions for framing.

The papers of the Duke of Wellington are at Southampton University and there is a fully searchable database at www.archives.lib.soton.ac.uk/wellington.shtml. A selection of despatches and letters from the Duke can also be found at www.wtj.com/archives/wellington.

An attractive site devoted to the Peninsular War, describing many of the battles, is at www.peninsularwar.org/penwar_e.htm. And www.georgianindex.net/peninsularWar/ordersofbattle.html contains orders of battle for the British Army in the Peninsular, pages of history and a description of how the Army was organised.

A succinct introduction to the Battle of Waterloo can be found www.britishbattles.com/waterloo/waterloo-army-positions.htm.

The Regency rake Captain Gronow's eyewitness account of the battle can be read at www.eyewitnesstohistory.com/waterloo.htm, and that of a Scottish cavalryman, Corporal Dickson, at http://chnm.gmu.edu/revolution/d/529.

An excellent interactive game allowing the visitor to refight the Battle of Waterloo is at www.bbc.co.uk/history/british/empire_seapower/launch_gms_battle_waterloo.shtml.

Ian Fletcher runs regular tours to the battlefields of the Peninsular and Waterloo. More can be found on his informative site at www.ifbt.co.uk. Details of tours specific to Waterloo are at http://waterloobattletours.users.btopenworld.com/index.html.

In 1907 the historian G Macaulay Trevelyan considered what might have happened had Napoleon had won, his analysis is posted at www.geocities.com/Athens/Forum/7227/ifnapwon.htm. After all, Wellington famously commented that 'it has been a damn close run thing'.

In Britain the ill-fated war against the United States (1812–1815) has almost been forgotten. However, in North America – particularly Canada, which successfully resisted an American invasion – the War is regarded as a key event in the nation's development. As a result there are a number of interesting sites, such as www.warof1812.ca, which has a lot about British military stationed in Canada during the war (and gives you the opportunity to buy a reproduction flintlock rifle), and www.galafilm.com/1812, which, although aimed more at schools, has some interesting pages for adults.

Another excellent site is www.militaryheritage.com/1812.htm, with many articles about the British Army in North America, eyewitness accounts and explanations of battles (from the British perspective). An American site with descriptions of battles and campaigns is www.mywarof1812.com.

Crimean War

The Crimean War took place between 1854 and 1856, largely on the Crimean Peninsula, although there was considerable naval activity in the Baltic. It is remembered today for an act of reckless heroism – the Charge of the Light Brigade – and the poor treatment of soldiers by the British War Office and senior officers in the field, particularly with regard to medical care, which was, as popular myth has it, only resolved by the 'lady with the lamp', Florence Nightingale. The truth, as these websites suggest, was somewhat more complicated:

The Crimean War Research Society at www.crimeanwar.org has much of interest, with FAQs (frequently asked questions) about the war and a chronology of events.
Two fairly detailed and largely complementary sites about the war are www.batteryb.com/crimean_war, which has a military bias, and www.victorianweb.org/history/crimea/crimeaov.html, for the social and political side.

The conduct of the war was exposed largely in reports for *The Times* and other newspapers. A selection of these, together with Parliamentary papers and memoirs are available at www.crimeantexts.org.uk. And www.silverwhistle.co.uk contains the diary of Fanny Duberley, the wife of a Crimean War officer, plus extracts from cavalry training manuals written by Louis Edward Nolan (1818–1854). The diary of Charles Underwood, a private in the 19th Foot (Green Howards), can be found at www.greenhowards.org.uk/gh-diaries/charlieusherwood.htm.

The war was the first to be photographed, most famously by Roger Fenton. A set of his extraordinary photographs are at www.loc.gov/rr/print/coll/251_fen.html.

www.chargeofthelightbrigade.com tells the story of the Charge of the Light Brigade with details of the men who took part. A radio interview with historian Terry Brighton about the Charge of the Light Brigade is at www.npr.org/templates/story/story.php?storyId=4123120.

www.histdoc.net/lauttasaari/crimean.html is a Finnish page devoted to the Anglo-French bombardment of the Russian fortress of Sveaborg, south of Helsinki, in 1855.

An interesting if rather opinionated, site about Florence Nightingale is at www.florence-nightingale-avenging-angel.co.uk. Another by the American singer Country Joe Macdonald is at www.countryjoe.com/nightingale – you can even book him to perform at a gig. In addition there is an excellent small museum devoted to her life at St Thomas's Hospital in London: www.florence-nightingale.co.uk.

Colonial Wars

Sometime's described as Queen Victoria's Little Wars, the British Army was engaged in many campaigns in the decades after the Crimean debacle. With the exception of temporary reverses at the hands of the Zulus in 1879, and more seriously the Boers in 1882, they were all easy victories. And as such they resonated with the increasingly patriotic British public, and still have a ring in these rather less certain days:

Kevin Asplin's http://hometown.aol.co.uk/kevinasplin/home.html with a huge range of medal rolls, muster lists and other information. Initially it concentrated on the Boer War, but it has subsequently broadened out to cover the whole of the latter half of the nineteenth century. It might not look pretty, and navigation is pretty basic, but it is a superb resource. So good, indeed, that I have included it in my top ten websites for military history (see p. 204).

www.members.dca.net/fbl is, in some ways, not a dissimilar site, although it is not comprehensive and has not been updated since 2003. The highlights are perhaps the collection of photographs of British and Indian soldiers.

www.britishempire.co.uk is a superb site about the British Empire in the nineteenth century, with some interesting pages on the military aspects (both Army and Navy).

http://homepage.powerup.com.au/~qdeck/navy.htm is the home page for the Queensland Naval Brigade re-enactors. There are pages about the original Naval Brigade, which saw service during the Boxer Rebellion and the Boer War.

An excellent site devoted to the wars with the Maoris of New Zealand between 1845 and 1872 is www.newzealandwars.co.nz. There are pages on causes, campaigns and consequences. A more specialist site is www.atonz.com/genealogy/nzdefence.html, which looks at British forces recruited from the settlers.

http://hicketypip.tripod.com is the website of a Kiwi re-enactment group based on the 65th Regiment, which was stationed in New Zealand between 1860 and 1870. The site features a replica of a contemporary drill manual.

The Zulu War (1878–1879) has always attracted researchers, particularly the heroic stand at Rorke's Drift on 22 January 1879, which saw the award of more Victoria Crosses than any other action in the history of the British Army. The story is told at www.rorkesdriftvc.com.

www.genealogyworld.net/azwar/index.html has a number of pages relating to the Zulu War and the people who fought in it. It includes a roll of all the men at Rorke's Drift. www.zuluwar-usuthu.com is an interesting site with lots of information. It is basically for re-enactors but there are details of the descendents of men who were at Rorke's Drift and Isandhlwana.

www.1879memorials.com/index.html is a somewhat eccentric site, tracing memorials of the men who fought during the war. So far they have identified 1,440 memorials and graves.

Ian Knight is a world expert on the Zulu War of 1878–1879, so his website www.kwazulu.co.uk, is a good place to find out more about an iconic episode in British Army history. And if you are researching the war then you should join the Anglo-Zulu War Historical Society at www.anglozuluwar.com.

The Second Afghan War took place between 1878 and 1880. www.garenewing.co.uk/angloafghanwar features a history of the war with a database describing many of the participants.

There are two American companies making and selling replicas of the kit worn by soldiers of the late Victorian Army at www.regimental-quartermaster.com and www.britishmilitaria.com. The prices seem very reasonable.

Anglo-South African War 1899–1902

The Boer War, as it is more commonly called, was, at its simplest, a war of imperial greed. The British coveted the diamonds and gold found on the Rand, which were controlled by the independent Transvaal Republic. As is so often the case in British military history, the commanders seriously underestimated the strength, skills and will of the enemy.

The war itself is divided into two parts – the first saw a series of British reverses, most notably the sieges at Ladysmith and Mafeking, followed by the arrival of reinforcements and a change in strategy and the fall of the Boer capitals of Bloemfontein and Pretoria in June 1900. The second saw a long-drawn-out guerrilla war by gangs ('commandos') of lightly armed and highly mobile Boers and the introduction of the first concentration camps housing women and children, designed to cut support to their menfolk. This brutal but effective policy eventually forced the surrender of the commandos in June 1902. Britain was aided by her colonies in Australia, New Zealand and Canada, which sent troops to help, and a number of regiments were raised in South Africa itself:

An interesting general introduction to the war is provided by the Anglo-Boer War Philatelic Society at http://www.boerwarsociety.org/Outline.cfm. And a variety of articles on the Boer War can be found at http://africanhistory.about.com/od/angloboerwar/AngloBoer_War_18991902.htm.

Images of Boer War artefacts found in Welsh museums are at http://www.gtj.org.uk/en/subjects/288.

If you are just interested in researching men who served in the Boer War, www.genealogyworld.net/boer/index.html is a good place to start. My page at www.sfowler.force9.co.uk/page_20.htm also describes sources for researching British soldiers, particularly at TNA, although it is rather dated.

www.pcansr.net contains a database of nurses who served during the conflict, with some information about nursing services during the period. A list of volunteer nurses from the Australian colony of Victoria is given at http://users.westconnect.com.au/~ianmac/nurses.html.

Details of 24,000 British soldiers who died during the war are at http://www.roll-of-honour.com/Databases/BoerDetailed/index.html. Most deaths were the result of sickness, not enemy action. Lists of men who appear on war memorials in East Anglia, compiled by the Cambridgeshire Family History Society, may be found at www.cfhs.org.uk/BoerWarDeaths.

Another database is the OZ-Boer Database at http://members.pcug.org.au/~croe/ozb/oz_boer0.htm, which includes details of Australian troops in South Africa, many of whom would have been born in the British Isles. A related site is Defending Victoria http://users.netconnect.com.au/~ianmac/boermain.html, which is devoted to men from the Australian colony of Victoria who fought in the war.

Extracts from the diary of Private J W Milne, Gordon Highlanders, is at www.jwmilne.freeservers.com.

The Siege of Ladysmith is described at http://ladysmith.kzn.org.za/ls/42.xml, with a list of British units present. A short article accompanied by photographs of Intombi Hospital, on the outskirts of the town, can be read at http://rapidttp.com/milhist/vol056sw.html.

A contemporary article from the *Manchester Guardian* on the Battle of Spion Kop is at http://century.guardian.co.uk/1899–1909/Story/0,94838,00.html.

http://library.thinkquest.org/26852/begin.htm is a South African site devoted to the Siege of Mafeking, 1899–1900.

Pages from a diary kept by an African resident, Sol T Plaatje, dispel the myth that it was just a white man's war. The native population suffered rather more than the whites: see www.museumsnc.co.za/mcgregor/departments/history/blacksinwar/mafsiege/mafeking.htm. Another South African to keep a diary was William Robertson Fuller, Protectorate Regiment, which can be read at: http://usscouts.org/usscouts/history/siegediary.html.

William McGonagall's poem celebrating the lifting of the Siege is at www.mcgonagall-online.org.uk/poems/mpgmafcking.htm. He is generally reckoned to be one of the worst Victorian poets, and yet remains endearingly popular.

Extracts from many books of the period can be downloaded from the attractively designed http://pinetreeweb.com/perspectives.htm. You can down a contemporary *Handbook of the Boer War* from www.gutenberg.org/etext/15699.

About an hour of existing film footage of the War exists. The National Film Archive catalogue of what survives is at www.bfi.org.uk/nftva/catalogues/catalogue/2.

The Boer War, from the perspective of the Boers themselves, is told at http://web.archive.org/web/20060509235230/http://abw.netfirms.com/index.html. The Anglo-Boer War Museum in Bloemfontein was initially opened to present the Boer perspective: see www.anglo-boer.co.za.

A comprehensive site about the colony of Victoria during the war is at http://users.westconnect.com.au/~ianmac/site.html.

www.lighthorse.org.au/toc.htm is dedicated to the Australian Light Horse, which served in the Boer War and the First World War, and features pages relating to the regiment's modern-day successors.

www.warmuseum.ca/cwm/boer/boerwarhistory_e.html has pages about the Canadian involvement in the war.

India

The British were involved militarily in India from the early seventeenth century until the last troops left after independence was granted to India and Pakistan in August 1947. In addition to British Army regiments and other units, there was the Indian Army, under the command of the Viceroy and led by British officers.

http://members.ozemail.com.au/~clday/regiments.htm is an excellent general site about the British in India. On the regiments' page are details of regimental histories for units which served on the subcontinent, rolls of honour and descriptions of actions (mainly relating to the nineteenth century).

The Asia, Pacific and Africa Collection at the British Library maintains the records of the old India Office and Library, which contain many records about the British in India and the Indian Army before 1947. There are some finding aids at www.a2a.org.uk and you can download leaflets at www.bl.uk/collections/orientaloffice.html.

The Families in British India Society (FIBIS) has an on-line guide to researching ancestors who were in the Indian armed forces at www.fibis.org.

www.wewerethere.mod.uk contains an on-line exhibition on the participation of ethnic minorities in the armed forces since the 1750s, with some nice pictures.

www.eicships.info is a database and related information about merchant ships of the East India Company, which sailed between Britain and India from 1600 to 1834.

A detailed page on the Indian Order of Merit, awarded between 1837 and 1847, is at http://faculty.winthrop.edu/haynese/india/medals/IOM/IOM.html. There is no list of recipients. The same webmaster also has pages on the medals issued by the Honourable East India Company at http://faculty.winthrop.edu/haynese/india/medals/EICMed.html.

A general site about the Indian Army in the nineteenth century (but with an emphasis on medals) may be found at www.members.dca.net/fbl.

www.king-emperor.com is an attractive website devoted to the Indian Army between 1901 and 1939 with lots of articles, information and photos. However, it does take a long time to load, particularly if you do not have a broadband connection.

The website of the Indian Centre for Military History – www.indianmilitaryhistory.org – has many articles on the Indian Army, including miscellaneous orders of battle.

www.bharat-rakshak.com/LAND-FORCES/Army/Conflicts.html is a collection of photos and pictures of the Indian Army from the 1760s until the present day. Perhaps of more interest are the photographs taken by John Walter Wright of the Bedfordshire Regiment, while stationed in India during the First World War, at http://uk.geocities.com/india1914.

www.bacsa.org.uk is the website of the British Association for Cemeteries in South Asia, which attempts to preserve the records and the cemeteries themselves. The site contains a few useful resources.

An incomplete database of cemeteries in India and Pakistan, accompanied by photographs, can be found at www.indian-cemeteries.org. If you are researching the area around Bangalore, www.geocities.com/Athens/Acropolis/9460/index.html offers a memorial to British soldiers who died there, and features plenty of photos.

Chapter 9

FIRST WORLD WAR – INTRODUCTION

'The War to End all Wars' began, for the British Empire at least, on 4 August 1914 and formally ended with the signing of the Treaty of Versailles almost exactly five years later on 28 June 1919, although, of course, the fighting actually finished on 11 November 1918.

The war was one of attrition, of industrial powers locked in mortal combat, waging a total war designed to exhaust the enemy's military and economic resources. Britain and her allies won because they successfully bled Germany dry, thanks to four years of meat-grinding battles on the Western and Eastern Fronts, and a now almost forgotten naval blockade, which prevented foodstuffs and raw materials reaching an increasingly hungry population.

As a result, the First World War was probably the first event in British history to affect every man, woman and child. Men were conscripted, women worked in factories and had to deal with rationing, while children learnt about the war in classrooms and collected eggs for wounded soldiers.

The terrible cost of the war in lives lost cast a long shadow over the following decades. A shadow that is still perceived today, as demonstrated by the massive rival of interest over the last decade or so, illustrated by the growth of battle tours of the Western Front, the study of the war poets, and the genealogical research into ancestors who were willing – or unwilling – members of the armed forces.

Background information

There are a number of sites providing background information about the war. Because the First World War is a key part of the National Curriculum, they are often written with schools in mind.

www.nationalarchives.gov.uk/pathways/firstworldwar/index.htm provides comprehensive introduction to history of war, largely for schools, but there is an interesting page about service records and how two-thirds came to be destroyed in 1940. Another general schools site is www.channel4.com/history/microsites/L/lostgeneration/index.html.

More interesting is the 'walking with ghosts' website at www.ww-ghosts.com/html-files/introduction.htm, which was prepared by the Green Howards regimental museum for local schools, although it offers a general introduction to the technology of the war and how it affected people's lives.

Diaries and papers of 2nd Lieutenant Cecil Slack, East Yorkshire Regiment, are at www.greatwar.eril.net/default.htm, with activities for school students undertaking Key Stages 2 and 3.

http://fallenheroes.moonfruit.com is a project by staff and pupils at Tideway School in Newhaven, who created the site to display the results of the students' research following their visits to the Western Front. It includes research guides and scans of an old photograph album, which had been bought by a teacher.

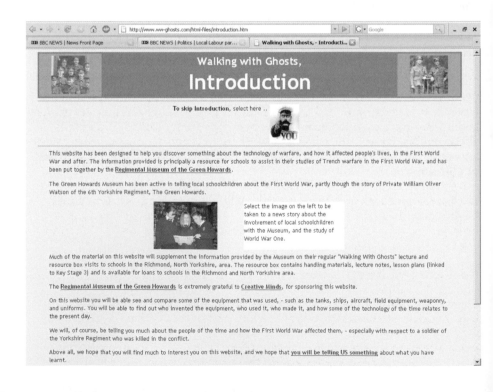

In addition, there are several sites that appeal to both schools and the general visitor. I liked the now rather dated http://news.bbc.co.uk/1/hi/special_report/1998/10/98/world_war_i/197437.stm, which was originally prepared for the 80th Anniversary of the Armistice in 1998, and offers a number of general pages about the war, including a selection of letters home and a story about clearing 'the harvest of death' – the munitions constantly found by farmers today along the former Western Front. Another similar site is www.firstworldwar.com, which features a number of unusual articles on aspects of the war and its aftermath. At the time of writing, recent postings had been on Hitler's experience of the trenches and the Memorable Order of Tin Hats, a veterans' association.

Trenches on the Web, at www.worldwar1.com, is one of the largest (and oldest) websites online. It is massive American site devoted to all the combatants, with photographs, posters and reminiscences. There are also links to over 600 websites devoted to all aspects of the war.

Strangely one of the best introductory sites is provided by a neutral: www.worldwar1.nl is a Dutch site with hundreds of links to other sites about the war.

Documents And Images Online

There are a number of on-line collections of documents and images, such as original photographs and posters:

One of the best collections is provided by Brigham Young University at www.lib.byu.edu/~rdh/wwi, with links to many other sites, including the University of Wisconsin, which has a selection of Bruce Bairnsfather cartoons taken from the *Fragments from France* series of booklets, plus propaganda about the British war effort in Danish. There also lots of scanned documents about the war, many of which are very unusual, plus links to other websites of interest.

www.greatwardifferent.com is a site containing extracts from British and Continental newspapers and magazines of the period, mainly about life experienced by civilians. There are many stories that offer a new light on the conventional histories of the war.

www.art-ww1.com/gb/peintre.html is an interesting site showing examples of First World War art from across Europe. It is arranged by artist. A French site (in French) showing some of the work of French artists is at http://dessins1418.free.fr.

www.library.georgetown.edu/dept/speccoll/britpost/britpost.htm is a small on-line exhibition mainly of British recruitment posters. For a similar collection of American posters, visit www.library.georgetown.edu/dept/speccoll/amposter.htm.

Still very much a work in progress, but when complete, www.ww1-propaganda-cards.com/index.html will contain images of nearly 2,500 propaganda postcards produced by both sides during the war with explanatory text.

Tracing Soldiers

The Long, Long Trail at www.1914–1918.net has many excellent pages on tracing ancestors who served in the British Army, explaining how to begin the search. There are also orders of battle (ORBAT), extracts from war diaries and biographies, so you can get an idea of what it was like in the trenches. The webmaster, Chris Baker, runs a professional research service at www.1914–1918.org and a forum for debate about the Great War at www.1914–1918.invisionzone.com/forums.

Although dated, www.rfc-rnas-raf-register.org.uk has some useful tips about researching men who fought in the war, particularly in the Royal Flying

Corps. The webmaster, David M Barnes, is compiling a database of everybody who served in the Royal Flying Corps/Royal Naval Air Service and RAF during the war. He also offers a service identifying soldiers in old photographs.

www.members.aol.com/deathpenny1 attempts to match up death plaques (known as dead men's pennies) with the descendents of the men who originally received them.

www.burnleyinthegreatwar.info is a splendid site about Burnley and the men who went away to fight, including lists of all who served.

The small West Sussex village of Chailey played a full part in the war, as www.chailey1914–1918.net shows. At its heart are biographies of men from the village who fought, and 54 VAD nurses who served in a military hospital in the village. There is also a blog by the webmaster (as well as another he posts about life in India, where he now lives).

http://www.leeds.gov.uk/page.aspx?egmsIdentifier=fcc07d76-c701-49c3-acc3-4384d38390b3 is a database of the Absent Voters electoral registers for Leeds, containing names of the city's men who were in the services in late summer of 1918.

www.geocities.com/athens/pantheon/3828/ tells the story of Scottish professional football players who joined up, particularly those from the Heart of Midlothian club in Edinburgh.

There are several sites devoted to the men from British and Commonwealth forces who were 'shot at dawn' for various crimes, including cowardice in the face of the enemy, desertion and murder. The campaigners point out that many of the individuals were suffering from shell-shock or a mental breakdown and should have been referred for psychiatric help:

www.shotatdawn.org.uk was the website for the body that campaigned successfully for a pardon to be a granted to the men. There is a lot of interesting background material, with a list of the men who were executed. Unfortunately, at time of writing, the website seems to have closed and you may need to use the Internet Archive (www.archive.org) to access the resources that were formerly on the site. If you are interested in where the executed men in the Ypres Salient are buried, www.users.globalnet.co.uk/~dccfarr/sad.htm will tell you.

Websites about men shot at dawn of Irish birth can be found at http://shotatdawncampaignirl.org, and those of Welsh extraction at www.shotatdawnwales.org.uk. Finally, http://home.cogeco.ca/~cdnsad is about the 23 Canadian soldiers who were 'shot at dawn'.

Blogs

Probably the best blog on the period is 'Trench Fever' at
http://trenchfever.wordpress.com. It is by Dr Dan Todman, Queen Mary
University of London, and is really about the strategic and military side of
the war and strays into discussing military history in general. His earlier
postings can be found at http://trenchfever.blogspot.com – there are no links
between the two sites. Victoria's Cross at http://victoriacross.wordpress.com
is another blogger looking at twentieth-century military history in general.
Other blogs include:

- http://greatwarfiction.wordpress.com, which discusses literature of
  the First World War.

- Another literary blog is http://only2rs.wordpress.com.

- Meanwhile, 'Break of Day in the Trenches' at
  www.whatalovelywar.co.uk/war has notes on the blogger's research
  into 'The First World War and Popular Culture' with a lot more
  besides.

- An Australian blogger discussing, mainly Australian, aviation
  history of the period is at www.australianflyingcorps.org.

- Not really a blog, but a forum,
  http://1914–1918.invisionzone.com/forums is one of several places
  about the First World War where you can ask questions or take part
  in debates about the war and its conduct.

Battlefield Tourism

There has been a huge increase in tourism to the Western Front over the past
two decades or so. With the Channel Tunnel and an impressive motorway
network, it is now an easy day trip from London. The roads are generally
good and the major attractions easy to find, with a range of hotels, bars and
restaurants to suit most pockets. There are a number of companies that
organise tours, but it is perfectly possible to construct your own itinerary.
The sites here offer some guidance, as well as providing other information
about the Western Front, then and now.

Hellfire Corner at www.fylde.demon.co.uk/welcome.htm has an off-putting
home page, but many articles about visiting the Western Front, war
memorials, tracing individual soldiers, as well as links to the webmaster's
military bookshop.

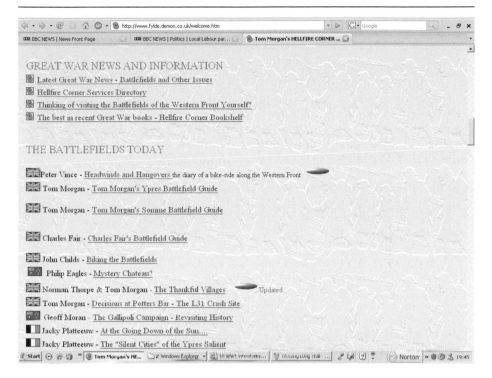

www.ww1battlefields.co.uk has pages about travel to the Western Front today, but is perhaps best for the pages of reviews of books about the war.

www.battlefield-tours.com is mainly a site for a battlefield tours company, but there are some additional interesting pages relating to the Somme and Ypres.

If your interest is the Somme rather than Flanders, the www.somme-battlefields.co.uk/en is a good place to start, with plenty of advice for potential visitors. While there, one place you must visit is Avril Williams' B&B and tearoom at Auchonvilliers on the Somme: details at www.avrilwilliams.com. While there, make sure you visit the cellar with its original wartime graffiti.

Phil Curme visits battlefields (not just First World War ones) on holiday. www.curme.co.uk/index.htm contains his holiday snaps and musings. It's better than it sounds!

Although hard to read, http://user.glo.be/~snelders/contents.html is an excellent practical site about Gallipoli, how to get there, and what to see when you do. There are lots of pages about the campaign, such as the weather, and notes of a visit to the peninsula in 1934.

Miscellaneous Sites

www.thegreatwarsociety.com describes Britain's premier re-enactment society for the period of the First World War. Members (and anybody else for that matter) can buy replicas of equipment, munitions and even stationery of the period at www.tommyspackfillers.com/gallery/gallery.php.

www.greatwar.nl is a Dutch site with some thought-provoking articles and many collections of superb photographs. For example, there's a scary article about the munitions dumped in the North Sea in 1919 and what could happen to it.

www.geocities.com/wwihorse is an excellent site devoted to the role of horses in the First World War (as well as a Second World War home front re-enactment group), with many interesting pages. Unfortunately, it is no longer being updated. Also available at http://mysite.wanadoo-members.co.uk/wwihorse.

Two other webpages looking at animals and the war are www.firstworldwar.com/features/forgottenarmy.htm – about the experiences and treatment of British horses at the Western Front – and various pages from contemporary newspapers at www.greatwardifferent.com/Great_War/Animals_at_War/Animals_at_War_00.htm.

www.edithcavell.org.uk is about the life of Edith Cavell, the nurse from Norfolk who was executed by the Germans in October 1915 for helping escaped British prisoners of war in Brussels. For many years it was claimed that she was innocent, but recent research showed that she had links to British intelligence. Even so, she was a brave and humane woman, as this site shows.

Chapter 10

FIRST WORLD WAR – CAMPAIGNS AND BATTLES

Western Front

The Western Front meandered for over 600 miles between Nieuport on the Belgian coast and Pfefferhouse on the Swiss border. British interest largely lay in the 150 miles or so between Iepern (Ypres) and the Somme river in Picardy. It was here that most of the great battles of the war were fought: Ypres, Somme and Passchendaele are names still familiar to most people. And if the argument about lions led by donkeys is somewhat simplistic, it is true that hundreds of thousands of young men from both sides fell fighting for nothing but a few yards of mud. Their remains lie at rest in cemeteries, large and small, which are scattered over the flat countryside.

The Western Front Association exists to study the First World War in France and Flanders. Their website, http://w3.westernfrontassociation.com has some excellent resources, including (unusually) reviews of books, as well as details of events at local branches and links to other sites. If you are at all interested in the First World War then you should join.

www.greatwar.co.uk/index.htm provides a clear introduction to the major battles at Ypres and the Somme, as well as other themes of the war. It might be a useful resource for older schoolchildren and undergraduates.

The Long, Long Trail www.1914–1918.net has many excellent pages on tracing ancestors who served in the British Army. There are also ORBATs, extracts from war diaries and biographies, so you can get a feel of what it was like in the trenches. The webmaster, Chris Baker also runs a professional research service at www.1914–1918.org.

The Old Front Line at http://battlefields1418.50megs.com is a clear and comprehensive site devoted to the Western Front (including Verdun) and

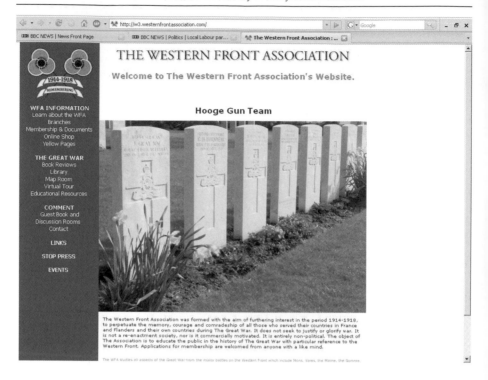

Gallipoli. There are many interesting pages and illustrations with tips for potential tourists and genealogists.

www.christmastruce.co.uk is an excellent site devoted to the famous Christmas truce of 1914. Of particular interest are transcripts of letters sent home describing the truces, which were published in local papers. www.nationalreview.com/weekend/history/history-weintraub122201.shtml is an interview with author, Stanley Weintraub, about his book on the Christmas Truce of 1914.

www.unfortunate-region.org is a slightly strange Dutch website with many interesting pages and many photographs of the Western Front as it is today. There are, for example, pages about the 'harvest of death' – the munitions that are still found by farmers even today.

Sadly all in French, http://monsite.wanadoo.fr/arham is about archaeology along the Western Front in France, and clearly warrants further exploration.

Photographs And Maps

www.westernfrontphotography.com/main.php provides a collection of superb photos of Western Front taken by Mike St Maur Sheil as it was in 2006. A similar site is www.landskip.co.uk with atmospheric black-and-white photographs of Belgium, France (and the UK) taken by a modern photographer, Paul Lipscombe.

The American Keystone View Company published many stereoscopic slides of scenes from the Western Front (mainly the French sectors) during the four years of war. They can be viewed at www.geh.org/fm/st08/htmlsrc/keyswwi_idx00001.html#76:0147:0091.

An article on trench maps and their history can be found at www.great-war-trench-maps.com/watm.htm, with related pages at http://web.westernfrontassociation.com/thegreatwar/articles/trenchmaps/readtrenchmap.htm.

www.greatwardigital.com is a company selling digitised trench maps that can be used in GPS systems. They are in 3D, which looks very impressive. It is definitely a toy for the enthusiast who has everything! There is also a links page to tour companies who take parties to the Western Front.

Flanders, Ypres and Passchendaele

The English used in the website of the In Flanders Fields Museum in Ypres is somewhat strange, but the site is an introduction to a superb museum: see www.inflandersfields.be.

If you visit Ypres you should be at the Menin Gate at 8pm, where the Last Post has been sounded every night since 1927 (except during the years of the German occupation between 1940 and 1944). It is a very moving experience, silencing even groups of fractious teenagers. It is organised by the Last Post Association, whose website is www.lastpost.be.

The website at www.passchendaele.be is for the relatively new museum at Passchendaele, which commemorates the great battle of 1917 (sometimes referred to as the Third Battle of Ypres). There is a roll of honour of men who fought there, which has been submitted by visitors.

www.wo1.be/eng/mainnav.html is a Belgian tourist site with pages about the war in the Westhoek region around Ypres and Poperinge. There are also news stories and details of places to stay. In addition, there are interactive maps of the battlefields, then and now, but I couldn't make them work.

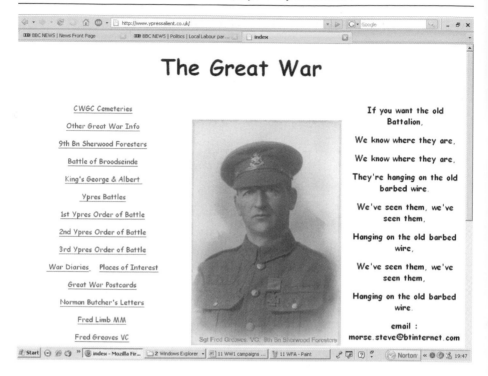

The Great War

CWGC Cemeteries

Other Great War Info

9th Bn Sherwood Foresters

Battle of Broodseinde

King's George & Albert

Ypres Battles

1st Ypres Order of Battle

2nd Ypres Order of Battle

3rd Ypres Order of Battle

War Diaries   Places of Interest

Great War Postcards

Norman Butcher's Letters

Fred Limb MM

Fred Greaves VC

Sgt Fred Greaves, VC, 8th Bn Sherwood Foresters

If you want the old Battalion,

We know where they are,

We know where they are,

They're hanging on the old barbed wire.

We've seen them, we've seen them,

Hanging on the old barbed wire,

We've seen them, we've seen them,

Hanging on the old barbed wire.

email :
morse.steve@btinternet.com

One man's exploration of the war his grandfathers saw in the Ypres salient is at www.ypressalient.co.uk. There is much to discover, including photographs of military graves, orders of battles, plus letters and diaries of trips to the front.

www.greatwar.co.uk/westfront/ypsalient/secondypres/index.htm is an interactive study of the Second Battle of Ypres in 1915. At present it is incomplete, but should become a very useful resource in time.

www.ypres-1917.com is a simple site by Paul Reed with information about the Battle of Passchendaele and what to see when you visit the area. There is a page devoted to some very attractive prints of some of the men and scenes of the battle by a modern artist, Søren Hawkes.

www.users.globalnet.co.uk/~dccfarr is an interesting site devoted to the battles and memorials fought around Ypres. Unfortunately, the choice of background makes it difficult to read the text.

Like so many researchers about the First World War, the webmaster of www.rleggat.com/ypres began by tracing an ancestor who died, but subsequently widened his interest to the battles themselves and the experiences of the men. The emphasis is on Ypres and the battles around the town.

www.ww1plugstreet.org is a site in French about the memorial at Ploegsteert on the Belgian–French border. The village was known to the Tommies as Plug Street.

France and the Somme

www.somme-1916.com is a Paul Read site devoted to the Somme with lots of information about the battle and what to see when you reach the area.

The Historial is an excellent museum at Peronne on the edge of the Somme battlefield, which is well worth visiting. Its website, www.historial.org/us/home_b.htm, also contains many interesting pages, particularly on cultural aspects of the war.

There is a new Thiepval Visitors Centre at the vast Thiepval Memorial, which commemorates 72,000 British and Commonwealth men who have no known grave. Details are at www.thiepval.org.uk.

The Somme Heritage Centre in County Down commemorates the 16th (Irish) and 36th (Ulster) Divisions and the sacrifices they made on the battlefield. Their website, www.irishsoldier.org, includes some resources, including material for researching the fallen.

http://freespace.virgin.net/sh.k/xvidiv.html tells the story of the 16th Irish Division, which was recruited from among the nationalist communities, decimated at the Somme and then forgotten by the Irish Republic until very recently.

www.nationalarchives.gov.uk/news/stories/118.htm?homelink=news is a summary of resources of The National Archives about the battle, including exhibitions and research guides.

www.gommecourt.co.uk is about the 56th Division and especially the London Scottish and their attempts to capture the village of Gommecourt on 1 July 1916.

Other Theatres Of Operations

The Gallipoli Association is devoted to the study of the campaign. The website at www.gallipoli-association.org contains a mass of useful information, including the ships involved in the landing and sets of brothers among the Allied troops. There are also numerous pages just for members.

www.richthofen.com/eef contains the official history of the campaign in Palestine in 1917 and 1918, first published in 1919. At the time of writing only a small part of the history is available online.

Transcripts of letters and other papers of T E Lawrence ('of Arabia'), including his book *The Seven Pillars of Wisdom* can be found at http://telawrence.net/telawrencenet/index.htm.

The Salonika campaign against the Bulgarians was one of the sideshows of the war. However, the Salonika Campaign Society exists to study it. Its website at www.salonika.freeserve.co.uk contains some useful background information.

www.salonika.freeserve.co.uk/NurseInSalonika.htm includes the biography of Nurse Edith Moor, with extracts from her diary.

Unit Histories

www.warpath.orbat.com provides an on-line order of battles for Allied formations. Although potentially useful it is hard to use, because it is not really arranged by unit, but by higher formation, generally division. Perhaps more useful are the ORBAT pages at www.1914–1918.net.

A small collection of regimental histories, including those for the 23rd Royal Fusiliers, Highland Light Infantry and 5th Battalion Leicestershire Regiment, are at www.bigenealogy.com/index.htm.

www.denniscorbett.com/241.html tells the story of 241 Brigade Royal Field Artillery (originally 2nd South Midland Brigade), which originally came from Worcestershire.

http://bedfordregiment.org.uk/index.html is a superb site telling the story of the Bedfordshire Regiment, arranged by battalion.

An unusual and thought-provoking site about the webmaster's research into a group photograph of officers from the 8th Berkshire Regiment, taken in 1915, and their descendents is at www.groupphoto.co.uk. The webmaster, Andrew Tatham, has made a film based on his researches, which clearly is worth seeing if it is shown near you.

www.royaldublinfusiliers.com consists of pages about the Royal Dublin Fusiliers between 1881 and 1922 (when it was disbanded), although at present it is mainly about the First World War.

One of the most famous units of the war was the Accrington Pals, the 11th (Service) Battalion (Accrington) East Lancashire Regiment, which was decimated on 1 July 1916. The deaths of so many men devastated the small mill town. All this is explained at www.pals.org.uk/pals_e.htm, which also includes film clips of the regiment marching through Blackburn.

www.greenhowards.org.uk/ww1-remembrance/html-files/ introduction.htm is a superb site dedicated to the Princess of Wales' Own Yorkshire Regiment, with a database of the men who appear on North Yorkshire war memorials.

www.huntscycles.co.uk is a comprehensive site dedicated to the little-known Huntingdonshire Cyclist Battalion, perhaps cruelly nicknamed the 'Gaspipe Cavalry'.

www.geocities.com/Athens/Acropolis/2354 is the website of a group of American re-enactors purporting to be men from the 7th Royal Irish Rifles. There are pages about drill and a rigorous dress code (the paragraph about watches is not for the politically correct!) and a number of general pages about the British Army of the period.

www.rimell.u-net.com/London%20Irish%20Diary.htm contains transcriptions of the war diary for the 20th London Irish (1/18th London Regiment) between 1916 and 1918. It is part of a wider side containing examples of military personnel records.

Material about the Queen's Own West Kent Regiment can be found at http://freepages.genealogy.rootsweb.com/~shebra/queens_own_royal_ west_kent_regiment.htm. You can download a regimental history covering the war period.

The Labour Corps has almost been forgotten. It was formed in 1917 and consisted of ex-front line soldiers who had been wounded or taken ill, plus men who, on enlistment, were found to be unfit for front-line service due to age or ill health. Its story is told at www.geocities.com/labour_corps.

A superb site is www.derbyshirelads.uwclub.net, which is mainly about men from Derbyshire who served in the war. There are also many pages about the county regiment – the Sherwood Foresters.

http://blackcountry-territorials.org is an excellent site about the 6th Battalion South Staffordshire Regiment, which contains a database with entries for more than 3,000 members of the battalion, as well as 60 more detailed biographies and extracts from the battalion war diary.

www.curme.co.uk/102.htm is a detailed site telling the story of 11 Battalion, Suffolk Regiment.

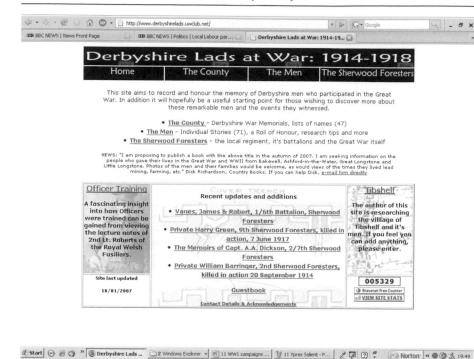

http://john-dillon.co.uk/yorklancs is about the York and Lancaster Regiment and the webmaster's grandfather Pte Patrick Dillon's service with it.

The Experiences Of Individuals

The websites below offer a surprisingly comprehensive insight into the war as seen by ordinary soldiers and their officers. Few of these accounts have been published, and most would have remained hidden in cupboards had they not been placed on the web. They are all fascinating, more often for the little details of everyday life in uniform rather than the descriptions of battles or fighting, which must have been difficult to describe in diaries (never mind the threat of the censor) or even remember after fifty or sixty years had passed:

www.addingham.info/war/brumfitt.htm contains a transcript of the diary kept by Corporal Brumfitt Atkinson, 19th Siege Battery, Royal Garrison Artillery for part of 1915 and 1916.

www.spoulton.fsnet.co.uk/Book/Index.htm tells the story of Private William Bentley, Hampshire Regiment, who was an ordinary soldier in India and later in France with letters and a rather overwritten biography.

www.borgognon.net/VEBdiary.html has the diary of Lt Victor Borgognon, Suffolk Regiment, for 1918, when he was stationed in Salonika. It is quite detailed and well written.

www.geocities.com/bradcrem/bradford_rbb_dli.html is about the Bradford brothers who served in the Durham Light Infantry, of whom Roland won the VC in France in 1916, and his brother Lt Commander George Nicolson Bradford, RN, won a VC at Zeebrugge in April 1918.

'The Boys from the Old Swan' at www.geocities.com/Heartland/Lake/6789 tells the story Harry Brown, 24 Royal Welch Fusiliers, Denbighshire Yeomanry, and his brothers from a pub in Wrexham and their experiences on the Western Front.

www.lib.byu.edu/~rdh/wwi/memoir/cairnie1917.htm contains the detailed and occasionally annotated diary of Lt John Bruce Carnie, King's African Rifles, for 1917. Other diaries for 1915, 1918 and 1919 are at www.lib.byu.edu/~rdh/wwi.

www.old-liverpool.co.uk/Carney.html has pages about Henry Carney, who served in the 15th Regiment in the 1860s, and his five sons, all whom joined the East Yorkshire Regiment and saw action in the Boer War and First World War.

The regimental surgeon of the 10th King's Liverpool Regiment, Noel Chavasse, VC and Bar, was one of the bravest soldiers (and most modest) to see action. His life is recorded at www.chavasse.u-net.com/chavasse.html.

www.culpitt-war-diary.org.uk contains the diary of Private George Culpitt, Royal Welch Fusiliers, between 1916 and 1918, with some background information about the man and his time in the Army.

www.users.globalnet.co.uk/~cjmorton/service.htm is about the career of Gunner Herbert Halliday, RFA, between 1914 and 1918 on the Western Front, where he was gassed, and in Salonika, where he contracted malaria.

http://web.ukonline.co.uk/xenophon/contents.htm has a transcript of the diary and written memoirs of Travis Hampson, RAMC, MC, who was a medical officer who saw service from mobilisation in August 1914 to the end of the war.

http://www.lib.byu.edu/~rdh/wwi/memoir/holmes.htm contains the diaries kept by Sapper Daniel Holmes, Royal Engineers, between 1916 and 1918.

http://www.pagebypagebooks.com/R_Derby_Holmes/ A_Yankee_in_the_Trenches/index.html is reproduction of an entertaining book *A Yankee in the Trenches* by R Derby Holmes of the Royal Fusiliers, first published in 1918. There is also a useful glossary of terms common in the British Army.

www.geocities.com/zippy_king2002 tells the story of Private Lionel Francis King, 6th Battalion, Essex Regiment, at Gallipoli and then in Palestine, with letters and photographs.

The diary kept by Sergeant Albert H Lewis MM, 216 Siege Battery, RGA, between 1916 and 1918 is at www.mikerlewis.com/diary.html. The site also includes additional material about the Battery.

http://met.open.ac.uk/group/jwL has the fascinating memoirs and photographs of Private George Linney, Royal Sussex Regiment, written in the months following the end of the war. The site also has material about the Home Guard and pages about historic military aircraft.

The unusually perceptive diary of Lt Robert Lindsay Mackay, MC, a medical officer with the 11th battalion, Argyll and Sutherland Highlanders, 1916–1918 can be found at http://lu.softxs.ch/mackay/RLM_Diary.html.

http://fredmitchell.mysite.wanadoo-members.co.uk/index.jhtml is about the career of Gunner Fred Mitchell, Royal Artillery, who served before and during the war, including some diaries for 1916.

'An ordinary hero' at www.carolenoakes.co.uk/ordinary.htm tells the story of Guardsman Frederick Elias Noakes of the Coldstream Guards. There are some fascinating things to be found here, including his views on smoking and drinking.

The Wilfred Owen Multimedia Digital Archive at www.hcu.ox.ac.uk/jtap includes poems and links to a small selection of newspapers published by the troops during the war. I particularly liked the *Daily Liar*, a satire upon the *Daily Mail*, which was hated by the troops for its jingoistic reporting of the war. At the time of writing the site was not responding.

'A Few of my Experiences whilst "On Active Service"' by Sapper Charles Rooke is at www.duffin.demon.co.uk/family/rooke.htm and covers the period between 1917 and 1918.

http://uk.geocities.com/britishimages shows the research carried out on several of the webmaster's ancestors who fought in the war, including 2nd Lt Sydney Sanders, 6th Btn Queen's Own (Royal West Kents) and Corporal James Hunt, Royal Engineers.

www.sassoonery.demon.co.uk has pages about the war poet Siegfried Sassoon.

Comprehensive diaries and papers of 2nd Lieutenant Cecil Slack, East Yorkshire Regiment, can be found at www.greatwar.eril.net/default.htm.

http://myweb.tiscali.co.uk/tedspires includes the diaries of Bombardier Bert Spires, MM 103 Brigade, Royal Field Artillery. He was at Ypres in 1917 and in Italy during 1918, and there are some sketches that originally accompanied the diary, as well as photographs and other material relating to his service.

http://www.censol.ca/research/greatwar/links.htm is devoted to the experiences of a Canadian officer, George van Wyck, MC, who served with the Tyneside Irish. There's a lot about the research undertaken into van Wyck's career.

Extracts from diaries of William Whitmore, 14th Royal Warwickshire Regiment (1st Birmingham Battalion), are at www.firstworldwar.com/diaries/whitmore.htm.

Chapter 11

SECOND WORLD WAR – INTRODUCTION AND CAMPAIGNS

If any war needed no introduction then the Second World War fits the bill. It is still part of British popular culture with exhibitions at museums, a constant stream of TV programmes and films, and a childish obsession in the tabloid press with reminding today's peaceful and democratic Germany of its Nazi past. And despite the war having ended over sixty years ago, dozens and dozens of books are published every year on all aspects, from general summaries of events to monographs on obscure aircraft and operations. It helps that, until very recently, so many veterans of the war were still around. They are now fading fast, but we all still know people who were there, like the extremely modest (and now rather deaf) father of a friend of mine who survived two tours of duty with 101 Squadron. Remarkably, until two years ago, all of his aircrew were still alive. This is reflected in the number of websites devoted to the war.

Background Information

As always, it is worth checking other sections of the book to see whether more general websites might be interest, but if you want some background information or to check a simple fact, www.secondworldwar.co.uk is a good place to start, with a general introduction to the war. Another good site is maintained by the BBC at www.bbc.co.uk/history/worldwars/wwtwo.

The Museum of WW2 is an American private museum devoted to the history of the war. You can take a virtual tour at http://museumofworldwarii.com.

More seriously and sensibly devoted to 'combating war by soundbite' www.ibiblio.org/hyperwar/UN/index.html is an American-centred site with lots of transcripts taken from official histories and the like. There is a lot of good stuff here, particularly on the diplomatic history of the war, but it can be hard to find.

www.euronet.nl/users/wilfried/ww2 has a day-by-day timeline of events during the war. Another timeline, and much more besides, including some simple maps of battles, can be found at www.onwar.com/index.htm.

There are, of course, a number of sites for schools and schoolchildren. One of the best is 'Heroes and Villains', which looks at some of the key decisions made during the war and the people who made them. It can be found at www.learningcurve.gov.uk/heroesvillains.

Spartacus is always a reliable source of historical information for schoolchildren and the Second World War pages are pretty comprehensive at www.spartacus.schoolnet.co.uk/2WW.htm. The BBC has a site looking at the experience of children during the war at www.bbc.co.uk/history/ww2children/index.shtml.

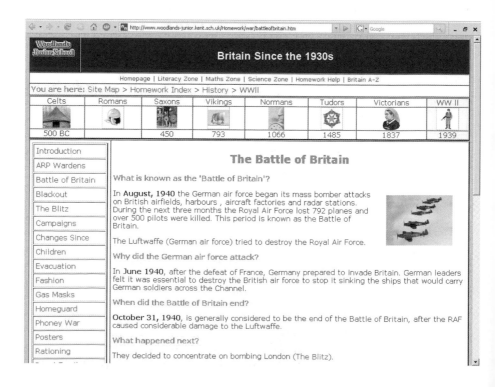

A site for teachers offering suggestions and resources can be found at www.tpyf.com/server/show/nav.00n00m001002001. One suggestion might be to set up a website devoted to the war, as the pupils of Woodlands Primary School in Tonbridge have at www.woodlands-junior.kent.sch.uk/Homework/Britain.html.

There are several blogs on the Second World War, including http://warstartsatmidnight.typepad.com, which mainly consists of reviews of books about the war. Wider ranging is http://militaryhistorythoughts.blogspot.com, although it is closely linked to the blogger's MPhil thesis on air power and the Dieppe Raid. Another blog, this time American, is www.ww2db.com, again with various pages on aspects of the war, particularly the war at sea.

www.geocities.com/Pentagon/Bunker/3351/index.html looks at the forgotten battles and events of the Second World War that don't always make the history books. Unfortunately it feels incomplete, but there are some interesting articles to be found here.

For light relief www.geocities.com/Pentagon/Bunker/3351/misc.html has a page of weird facts and coincidences. More along the same lines can be found at www.geocities.com/techbloke/limeydvr/facts.htm and www.secretsofworldwar2.co.uk.

Operations, Campaigns And Battles

Paul Read's excellent site at www.ww2battlefields.info claims to be the only introduction to the battlefields of the War (at least those engaged in by the Western Allies), and features a mass of information for researchers and tourists alike.

A real hotchpotch of articles on the operational history of the war, mixed up with material for wargamers, is at www.battlefront.co.nz.

Arnhem/Operation Market Garden

www.remberseptember44.com is a general site about the battle for Arnhem. Another general site is http://home.wxs.nl/~peter.vrolijk/ABRG.html, which contains pages provided by the Arnhem Battle Research Group. Unfortunately it is incomplete and works best in Internet Explorer.

Perhaps of more immediate use is www.nntk.net. It is an attractive site that provides some source material for the battle, plus a collection of photographs for the Battle of Crete in 1941. Another Dutch site is http://get-me.to/september1944 with a lot about the battle and the men who fought there. In addition, there are number of background pages: those about the divisions in Dutch society between the collaborators and the patriots are particularly interesting.

www.defendingarnhem.com is a fascinating Australian site on Arnhem from the German point of view. As the webmaster points out, this is a story which has rarely been told.

http://members.chello.nl/reinders2 is the well laid out history of an almost forgotten unit, 250 (Airborne) Light Composite Company, Royal Army Service Corps, which kept the men supplied with ammunition and provisions.

A detailed, if incomplete (and slow loading), site about British airborne forces during the Second World War is at www.pegasusarchive.org. There are many pages about Arnhem of course, but also other battles the troops participated in. A related general site on airborne forces with many pages on the 'Bridge too far' is at http://theairbornesoldier.com/index1.html.

D-Day and North West Europe

www.ccny.cuny.edu/library/Divisions/Government/DDay.html is an American university site offering links to other websites on D-Day. Unusually it is not overly biased towards the American perspective. Another introduction to the events of 6 June 1944 is provided by Encyclopaedia Britannica at http://search.eb.com/dday.

www.omaha-beach.org is a German website about the American beach at Omaha, although it is more about the webmaster's grandfather who commanded the German forces there. He also organises and runs battlefield tours to Normandy and the sites of the Franco-Prussian War of 1870.

If you intend to visit the beaches www.normandiememoire.com/NM60Anglais/nmeh/accueil.php is a useful place to start, with a mixture of tourist information and history designed for students.

One small battle took place near Gold Beach on 14 June in the village of Lingrevres. The story of the battle is told in an impressive website at www.glcoupar.freeserve.co.uk/battleoflingevres1944/index.htm.

www.oradour.info describes the background and events leading up to the destruction of the French village of Oradour-sur-Glane on 10 June 1944 by soldiers of the *Waffen-SS*, killing 642 men, women and children.

http://home.tiscali.nl/hgmkuip/blerick describes the 'perfect Battle of Blerick' (basically a small tank battle) that took place on 3 December 1944 in this Dutch village on the German border. The site commemorates the action with survivors' stories and photographs of the village, then and now.

Dunkirk

Considering how important the event was and its impact on the British psyche, there are surprisingly few sites devoted to the evacuation from Dunkirk in late May and early June 1940:

- http://www.theotherside.co.uk/tm-heritage/background/dunkirk1940.htm#visit is a rather unsatisfactory site with links to tourist sites. Of more use is www.dover-kent.co.uk/history/ww2b_dunkirk.htm, which is about Dover's role in the evacuation.

- www.ramsgatelifeboat.org.uk/dunkirk-evacuation.htm has pages about the role of lifeboats from Margate and Ramsgate in rescuing troops from the beaches at Dunkirk. The Association of Dunkirk Little Ships at www.adls.org.uk has pages about the little ships from all over South East England used in the evacuation.

Mediterranean and Italy

- www.geocities.com/techbloke is a Canadian site devoted to the 'forgotten campaigns' in Italy and the Pacific, but is rather more a collection of material about the war that interests the webmaster. There are a few clips from important radio broadcasts of the period.

- http://louishenwood.com/page01.html is devoted to the experiences of Malta and the Maltese during the siege of the islands in 1941 and 1942. Another site about the siege can be found at www.killifish.f9.co.uk/Malta%20WWII. Unfortunately, it is almost impossible to navigate around. Perhaps of more interest is www.merlinsovermalta.com, which describes the project to fly a Spitfire and Hurricane over Malta to mark the 60th Anniversary of the end of the Second World War in September 2005. There are also numerous pages about the island during the war.

- www.battleofmontecassino.com is a rather strange and incomplete site devoted to the Battle of Monte Cassino in 1944 and particularly the Polish troops who took part.

A site in Italian of photographs from the Italian campaign is at www.anpi.pesarourbino.it/fototeca2.php. Fortunately it is easy to work out and there are some interesting images available. Another Italian language site, this time less easy to use, is www.lacittainvisibile.it/storia.html, which looks at the experiences of civilians along the Gothic Line in 1943 and 1944.

South East Asia

www.burmastar.org.uk is the website of the Burma Star Association. There are many pages on the history of the campaign and the work of the Association.

www.rothwell.force9.co.uk/burmaweb/index.htm is another introductory site to the Burma campaign with some interesting pages. Unfortunately the intrusive background makes them hard to read.

An excellent site about the Chindits, who were British special forces operating behind Japanese lines in Burma in 1943 and 1944, is at www.chindits.info.

A project documenting the 1941 defence of Hong Kong is at www.hongkongwardiary.com. There is a list of members of the garrison and their fates until liberation in 1945. Also of interest is www.geocities.com/rcwpca, which is a moving site about the experiences of

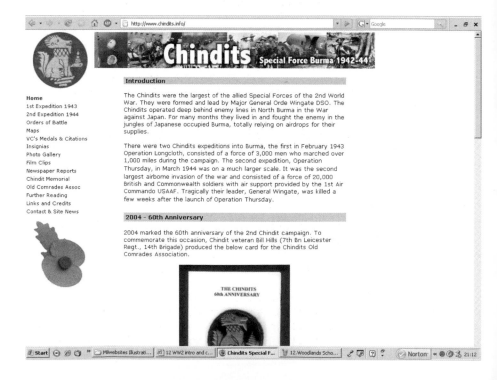

a battalion of the Royal Rifles of Canada captured during the surrender of Hong Kong in December 1941 and the webmaster's father, Major Maurice Parker, who was among their number.

www.hamstat.demon.co.uk contains pages about the webmaster's father's miraculous escape from Hong Kong in December 1941 with 2nd Motor Torpedo Boat Flotilla. Good *Boy's Own* stuff.

www.myfareast.org is mainly a history and travel site but there are introductory pages about the Japanese invasion of Malaya, as well as photographs of war memorials in Malaysia, Singapore and Thailand.

www.forcez-survivors.org.uk is an excellent site about the ill-fated Force Z, comprising HMS *Prince of Wales*, HMS *Repulse* and other ships, which were attacked by the Japanese off the coast of Malaya on 10 December 1941. There are casualty lists and eyewitness descriptions of the fateful last hours.

www.malayanvolunteersgroup.org.uk is a veterans' group for the mainly white Malayan Volunteers and their descendents. There is a summary of the history for the various units.

http://myweb.tiscali.co.uk/abeckett/pow/index.htm is mainly about the British communities in Indonesia and China before the war and their experiences under the Japanese. The usefulness of the site is somewhat marred by a migraine-inducing yellow background. Unfortunately the site was down in May 2007.

www.fortsiloso.com tells the story of Fort Siloso in Singapore, which was erected in 1878 and fell to the Japanese in February 1942. It has subsequently been restored.

http://pacific.valka.cz features the Naval War in the Pacific (mainly US and Japanese), with orders of battle, brief histories of ships and descriptions of operations.

Special Operations

http://alliedspecialforces.org is the website of the Allied Special Forces Association, which seeks to commemorate the work of the various special forces. There are many lists of men and women, but because of the weird use of frames, they are hard to use.

www.welfreighter.info tells the recently declassified story of the *Welfreighter*: a 37-foot-long miniature submarine, which was developed to land SOE agents on the coast of occupied Europe. Actually, there isn't very much about the submarine itself, but more about the other forms of landing agents by canoe or other miniature submarine.

www.64-baker-street.org is dedicated to the 39 women who served with the Special Operations Executive (SOE) and who were parachuted into France. No. 64 Baker Street was the wartime headquarters of SOE. Other sites of interest are: www.channel4.com/history/microsites/C/charlotte_gray/home.html, which tells the story of four female agents sent to France, and www.violette-szabo-museum.co.uk is devoted to an SOE agent Violette Szabo, GC, whose life was dramatised in the film *Carve Her Name With Pride*.

http://members.aol.com/HLarroque/sgbindex.htm offers a general introduction to SOE operations in France. www.soe-french.co.uk consists mainly of a list of agents sent to France by SOE's F Section. An academic study of the effectiveness of the Jedburgh teams, which were parachuted into France to train resistance groups in support of the US 12th Army in Normandy during the summer of 1944, is at www.cgsc.army.mil/carl/resources/csi/Lewis/Lewis.asp.

www.nederland4045.nl is the website of the Netherlands 1940–1945 Study and Living History Group, which aims to recreate the experience of wartime resistance.

www.shetland-heritage.co.uk/shetlandbus looks at the Shetland Bus, which ferried agents and others in and out of Norway.

http://users.pandora.be/ppa is a site devoted to No. 1 Demolition Squadron, better known as Popski's Private Army, which conducted special operations behind enemy lines in the Libyan Desert and later in Italy.

The almost forgotten story of SOE in the Far East, based on the wartime career of the webmaster's father, is told at www.btinternet.com/%7Em.a.christie. There is a lot of very interesting material to be found here, including downloadable radio interviews.

Prisoners of War

The National Ex-Prisoner of War Association for veterans and their families has a website at www.prisonerofwar.org.uk. There is little for the historian, although there is a list of POW camps.

The slightly disappointing site of the RAF Prisoners of War Society is at www.rafinfo.org.uk/rafexpow, although there is an inspirational page about Sgt 'Dixie' Deans, who organised British other rank prisoners at Stalag Luft III and elsewhere, and did much to keep morale high.

www.rafcommands.com/Air%20Force%20PoWs/RAF%20POWs%20Index.html has a roll giving details of all RAF prisoners of war. Names are generally correct at March/April 1944 with some entries being correct up to February 1945.

Prisoners of War – Europe

An excellent general site on British POWs with lots of photos and stories from some of the POWs themselves can be found at www.pegasusarchive.org/pow/frames.htm.

www.irishseamensrelativesassociation.org is devoted to Irish merchant seamen on British and Irish ships who became prisoners of war in Germany. They were held at Sandbostel, where some were tortured by the Gestapo.

It is claimed that over a million prisoners of war and concentration camp inmates were housed at Stalag XB at Sandbostel, near Bremen, at some stage during the war. An interesting German site about the camp and the prisoners is at http://gedenkstaette-sandbostel.de/englisch/homepage.htm.

Stalag VIIa at Moosburg in Bavaria housed American, French and Russian prisoners. www.moosburg.org/info/stalag/indeng.html offers a detailed site about the camp There is a useful links page.

www.merkki.com is an American site about Stalag Luft I at Barth, on the Baltic coast, which housed American and British airmen. Another site about

the camp with some photographs of what it looks like today is at
www.winternet.com/~stetrick/stalag-luft-one.html.

Prisoners of War – The Far East

www.cofepow.org.uk is website of the Children and Families of the Far East
Prisoners of War charity, which contains some useful research pages if you
are interested in researching an individual or a particular incident.

www.fepow-community.org.uk is an interesting site devoted to Far East
Prisoners of War with pages of research supplied by members. More about
researching the men can be found at www.researchingfepowhistory.org.uk,
as well as details of biannual conferences and regular seminars.

www.mansell.com/pow-index.html is a site devoted to Allied prisoners of
war in the Far East. There is an emphasis on American prisoners and camps.
The webmaster has rather alarming political views (at least to a European).

The Changi Murals were painted between 1942 and 1943 by a British Prisoner
of War, Bombardier Stanley Warren, of 15 Field Regiment, Royal Artillery in
the dysentery wing of the POW hospital.
www.petrowilliamus.co.uk/murals/murals.htm tells the extraordinary story
of how they were lost and then restored for all to admire.

www.changimuseum.com is the slow-loading site for the Changi Museum,
Singapore. There is a searchable database for 5,000 civilian internees.

One of the great crimes of the war was the construction of the
Burma–Thailand Railway, 'the Bridge over the River Kwai', in which 13,000
Allied POWs died (as well as perhaps 100,000 locals). www.pows-of-
japan.net looks at the men who were there. There is an emphasis on the
medical personnel. A Museum devoted to the building of the railway has a
website at www.tbrconline.com.

The Taiwan POW Memorial Society – www.powtaiwan.org/men.html –
includes a list of all the men (British, Commonwealth and American) who
were held by the Japanese on the island (once known as Formosa), as well as
pages about the camp conditions.

www.lisbonmaru.com is a site devoted to the tragic loss of the *Lisbon Maru*,
which was taking 1,800 British prisoners of war from Hong Kong to Japan in
October 1942 when it was sunk by an American submarine. Some 748 men
lost their lives.

Escape And Evasion

www.rafinfo.org.uk/rafescape is about the RAF Escape Society and the museum at East Kirby Aviation Museum in Lincolnshire. There is also a link to the equivalent American body.

www.conscript-heroes.com is a fascinating website, mainly about the Pat O'Leary Escape Line (or Pat Line) through France, based on the experiences of the webmaster's father, Peter Janes, although there is a lot more besides. A series of articles about the Pat O'Leary line and related subjects is at www.christopherlong.co.uk/pri/secpap.html.

The Escape Lines Memorial Society at www.escapelines.com has many pages about the escape lines and the brave men and women who assisted the escapers, often at great personal risk.

www.belgiumww2.info is a superb site telling the story of Allied escapers and evaders helped by the Comète Line in Belgium, which eventually took men across the Pyrenees to neutral Spain.

Mythologised by Hollywood, www.elsham.pwp.blueyonder.co.uk/gt_esc/index.html looks at the real 'Great Escape' from Stalag Luft III in March 1944.

Chapter 12

SECOND WORLD WAR – BRITISH ARMY AND ROYAL NAVY

British Army

Compared with the RAF (see next chapter), and to a lesser extent the Royal Navy (see below), life in the Army was generally not as obviously exciting, which may be why there are relatively few websites devoted to its activities during the Second World War. For much of the time between 1939 and 1945, the experience of war for many men was not one of daring deeds at 'the sharp end', but rather of a sedentary existence in camps or depots across the country, filling forms or passing ammunition to troops in the front line. In addition, the Army was made up of a much smaller proportion of men in uniform than had been the case in the First World War. Even so, in July 1945, just under 3 million men were serving in the Army, compared with 1 million in the Air Force, and 780,000 in the Royal Navy. An excellent introduction to the British Army during the War is at www.ww2battlefields.info, with a guide to tracing soldiers, orders of battle, and material about the landings in Normandy in 1944.

Orders Of Battle

Orders of battle (ORBATs) help identify the position of particular units at particular times. They can be of use to military historians and, especially, wargamers trying to understand how a battle or action was planned or conducted. As a result, there are a number of different sites offering ORBATs for the Second World War. Unfortunately, they are almost always incomplete or at best 'under construction'.

www.bayonetstrength.150m.com offers a simple introduction to the organisation of the armies of the major contestants, with a short introductory essay on the British Army during the war.

A bitter disappointment is http;//home.adelphia.net/~dryan67/orders/army.html, which offers ORBATs for British and Commonwealth forces, but for Britain there is just the order of battle of the Army in the UK in September 1939.

A related site is http;//homepages.force9.net/rothwell/index.htm, which is best for details of the lesser imperial forces for the first half of the war.

Another incomplete and hard to use site is www.ordersofbattle.com, which has some information about British Commonwealth, American and German units, their location and commanders.

Probably the best of all the sites is Leo Niehorster's at http;//niehorster.orbat.com/index.htm. It is hard to navigate, but there are some interesting pages. It's best to click on the 'What's New' button and scroll down to find what you want.

Armoured Vehicles

The British Army used a variety of armoured vehicles during the war. They were mainly inferior to those used by the Germans or even their American allies. It was not for nothing that German soldiers used to rather cruelly refer to the Churchill tank as being the 'Tommy cooker'.

The Tank Museum at Bovington in Dorset tells the story of tanks from the First World War to the present day. For a museum, a surprisingly large amount of useful material can be found on their website at www.tankmuseum.co.uk.

www.military-museum.org.uk is the website for the Newcastle Military Vehicle Museum, mainly contains Second World War equipment. Unfortunately, at the time of writing, the museum itself was closed for renovation work.

www.wwiivehicles.com offers basic information about the tanks used by the combatants.

The most important British tank of the war was the Churchill. www.armourinfocus.co.uk/a22 is devoted to the tank, with some crude but effective virtual pages showing the vehicle's interior.

The DUKW was developed by the Americans for the transportation of ammunition, supplies, troops, and equipment from supply ships offshore to fighting units on the beach. Some 2,000 were provided to the British and their story is told at www.dukws.co.uk.

Regimental And Unit Histories

http://hometown.aol.co.uk/asummerof44/myhomepage/collection.html tells the story of the Auxiliary Territorial Service for Women, with lots of material for collectors of ATS memorabilia and researchers.

The story of the 7th Armoured Division, nicknamed the Desert Rats, is comprehensively told at www.btinternet.com/~ian.a.paterson/main.htm. The division had an active history fighting in the Middle East, Italy and North West Europe.

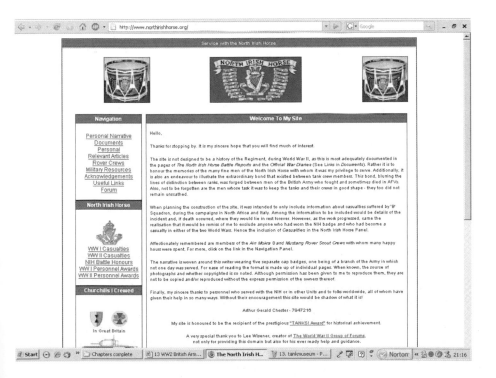

www.justordinarymen.org.uk is the website of the 1st Airborne Reconnaissance Squadron re-enactment group, with pages about the use of airborne forces during the war.

http;//theairbornesoldier.com/index1.html is a general site on British and American airborne units from the landings in Sicily and the Rhine crossings, but with an emphasis on Arnhem. A related site on airborne forces is www.pegasusarchive.org.

http;//16dli.awardspace.com – 16th Battalion, Durham Light Infantry, which served in Tunisia, Italy, Greece and Austria. The webmaster's father became an NCO in it. There is a useful page explaining the perennially thorny topic of Army service numbers.

www.gliderpilotregiment.org.uk – about the Glider Pilot Regiment, which guided the planes in which the airborne troops flew.

www.northirishhorse.org – information about the North Irish Horse, a battalion in the Royal Tank Regiment. The webmaster was a member, so there are also pages on his wartime experiences, although the HTML coding has rather gone astray. In addition, you can look at copies of war diaries, regimental magazines and other documentation.

For old gunners and students of the Artillery during the war http;//members.tripod.com/~nigelef/index.htm has much of interest. It is quite a technical account, however, with pages on fire planning and command and control.

The Experiences of Individual Soldiers

There a number of sites devoted to the stories of individual soldiers. In addition, www.unithistories.com has lists of officers from many countries arranged by unit and alphabetically, including promotions, theatres of operation and, occasionally, photographs. Together they give an idea of what it was like – the boredom and the friendship as well as fighting and the discipline:

http;//freepages.military.rootsweb.com/%7Eattwood/8thkri/index.htm is in memory of George William Attwood, 8th (Kings Royal Irish) Hussars who was killed in action on 14 June 1944 in Normandy. It includes a copy of the pamphlet *Tank Hunting*, which was issued to troops in 1940.

www.chindit.org.uk tells the extraordinary story of Sergeant William Clift, MM, who escaped from a Japanese POW camp in Rangoon, and later became a Chindit.

www.warlinks.com/jackcull/index.shtml looks at Signalman Jack Cull, who joined the Army as a regular in 1938, became involved in special operations and was involved in a mysterious raid on Yugoslavia in 1943.

www.geocities.com/sapper_dracuss is about Sapper Stanley Dracass, who was at D-Day. There are some interesting comments about discipline. Unfortunately, the background makes it hard to read.

www.alfgritton.co.uk has memories of Alf Gritton, Royal Tank Corps. It is largely based on interviews conducted a friend.

www.roymiddleton.btinternet.co.uk contains memories of Corporal Roy Middleton, 221 Field Coy, RE, who was at Dunkirk and in North Africa. There are also several pages containing reminiscences from other old engineers.

www.britain-at-war.org.uk/WW2/Alberts_Wa is about Albert Morrell, RAMC, who became a prisoner of the Japanese in 1942.

www.wargunner.co.uk tells the story of Gunner John Parsons, RA and Army Catering Corps. There are lots about the general experience of service in the Army during the Second World War, including pages on cooking.

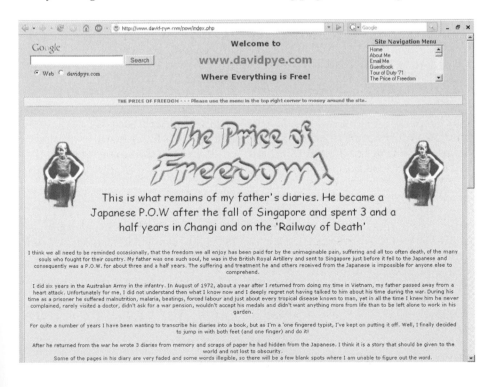

www.david-pye.com/pow/index.php is the diary and memoirs of webmaster David Pye's father, who was a Gunner and a prisoner of war in the Far East. Curiously, nowhere is the man's name given. There is lot of other good (non-military) stuff as well.

www.britishsoldier.com/ronindex.htm commemorates Troop Sergeant Ronald Tee, Reconnaissance Corps (Royal Armoured Corps).

www.irish-guards.co.uk contains the memoirs of Ivor White, Irish Guards, 1944–1948, including a page about his membership of the Home Guard.

Royal Navy

The Royal Navy during the Second World War played a huge role in keeping the sea lanes across the Atlantic free from enemy attack. But RN ships were involved in all theatres of operations, from fast torpedo boats attacking German shipping in the English Channel, and corvettes escorting supplies to the besieged island of Malta, to the Pacific Battle Fleet, which was assembled in the last months of the war to support the attack on Japan.

Background Information

Perhaps the best place to start researching the RN during the war is at www.naval-history.net – a superb introduction to the war at sea and the Royal Navy in particular. A recent addition is a detailed account of naval activities day by day, and a roll of honour of seamen who died in the service is promised shortly. There are also pages on the Navy from 1914 to the Falklands Campaign of 1982.

Another invaluable resource is devoted to the Fleet Air Arm – www.fleetairarmarchive.net/Index.html. The site includes histories of ships, squadrons, aircraft and a roll of honour for those who did not return. It is also clear and well designed.

Incidentally, if you are looking for more information about the FAA, it is worth exploring the sites on the Fleet Air Arm webring http://v.webring.com/hub?ring=fleetairarmwebri. The FAA Museum at Yeovilton (details at www.fleetairarm.com) is also well-worth visiting. It has a superb collection of aircraft and an excellent archive.

There are a couple of excellent sites about the almost forgotten Royal Naval Patrol Service (RNPS), which operated anti-submarine trawlers, and whose headquarters was at Sparrow's Nest, Lowestoft. The best place to start is at www.harry-tates.org.uk – there's even a short extract from a wartime film about their exploits. Their old comrades association is at www.rnps.lowestoft.org.uk, which also has some useful pages.

www.poulton.info/familyhistory/grimsby%20RNPSV.htm is a site designed around the memorial to the RNPS at Grimsby, which was unveiled in 2001. It has much about the Service at the port and the ships that were sunk on duty. Unfortunately it is slow to load, even with broadband.

For obvious reasons there are few re-enactors attempting to recreate life in the Royal Navy. However, although mainly a Napoleonic group, the Historical Maritime Society also has an interest in the Second World War, which you can read about at www.hms.org.uk/WWII/aboutuswwii.htm.

The Battle of the Atlantic

http;//uboat.net is a superb resource devoted to the U-boat, the war in the Atlantic and submarines in general, with histories of the U-boats and the ships that hunted them, as well as a day by day account of the battle.

www.mikekemble.com is a hotchpotch covering a variety of subjects, mainly – but not entirely – related to the Battle of the Atlantic. Also, it is rather strangely designed, but there is some good material to be found here.

www.3dhistory.de is an unusual site devoted to the recreation of a variety of battleships, including the *Bismarck, Admiral Graf Spee*, HMS *Hood*, and *Yamoto* in 3D graphics. It can be hard to find the images though.

Named Ships

www.hmsbarham.com is a site devoted to the battleship HMS *Barham* and the disaster in November 1941 that saw nearly 900 men lose their lives.

www.geocities.com/hmsdukeofyork contains pages on the history and crew of the battleship *HMS Duke of York*.

HMS *Edinburgh* was a convoy escort ship sunk while on a convoy to Russia in May 1942 with £40m in gold on board. Her story is told at www.hmsedinburgh.co.uk.

www.hmshood.com is the website for the old comrades association of the battleship HMS *Hood*, with lots about the ship's history and loss.

www.mikekemble.com/ww2/kite.html tells the story of HMS *Kite*, which was lost with all hands in August 1944 in the Arctic Sea. There is a roll of honour and pages on the history of the ship.

www.geocities.com/Pentagon/Quarters/4433 is about the battleship HMS *Rodney* and the webmaster's grandfather, who served onboard during the war. At the time of writing the website was down – temporarily, I hope.

www.hms-vengeance.co.uk is about HMS *Vengeance,* an aircraft carrier that served in the final few months of the war, and the Fleet Air Arm Squadrons that served on board. You will need to scroll down the page to get to the site proper.

www.hmswensleydale.co.uk/Frameset.htm is a fine and informative site about the destroyer HMS *Wensleydale,* which was largely engaged in operations in the English Channel and North Sea.
MTB 102 was the first motor torpedo boat bought by the Admiralty in 1937. Information about the vessel, and the attempts to preserve it, can be found at www.mtb102.com.

The Experiences of Individual Seamen

www.mikekemble.com/ww2/mgb.html is about the career of Able Seaman Norman Hine, DSM, who served aboard armed motor boats. There is much about the vessels themselves and the men who served upon them.

One man who lost his life in the last weeks of the war was Gus Holland, who was on MTB 494, which clashed with a German unit of MTBs off the Norfolk coast on 2 April 1945. His story, and that of the battle, is told at http;//home.it.net.au/%7Elambeth/mtb494.html.

Http;//home1.swipnet.se/~w-11578 is a site devoted to the naval career of the webmaster's father, Victor Johns, who served on a number of ships, including HMS *Resolution* and HMS *Vengeance.* There are also useful pages about researching the RN in the Second World War.

An interesting site is www.royal-naval-reserve.co.uk, which tells the story of the webmaster's grandfather, John Wilson, who served on trawlers in the Royal Naval Reserve, mainly out of Lowestoft.

Chapter 13

SECOND WORLD WAR - THE ROYAL AIR FORCE

With bravery (think Battle of Britain) and fast machines (think Spitfire) it is little wonder the RAF has long been a favourite subject for the enthusiast: consequently there is a large presence online. There are many websites, some of which are excellent, telling the story of the Royal Air Force, describing the men and the machines that took part, and providing information for researchers, enthusiasts and wargamers.

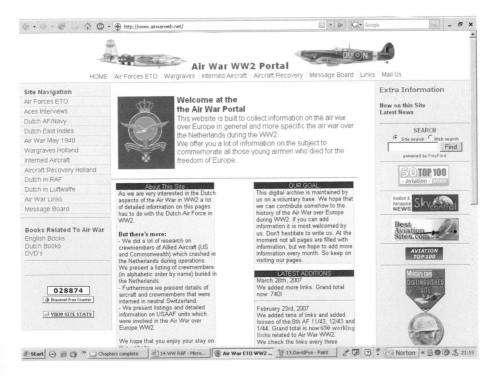

Background Information

A good place to start is the War Birds Resource Group at www.warbirdsresourcegroup.org, which is an American site offering information about the world's major air forces.

www.lesbutler.ip3.co.uk/tony/tonywood.htm provides detailed, but incomplete, databases and other resources relating to combat claims and casualties for the RAF, USAAF and *Luftwaffe*.

www.airwarweb.net is a comprehensive Dutch site devoted to the air war. It has lists of Allied and Axis planes interned in Switzerland. There are also some 700 links to other websites on the war in the air. Another site offering hundreds of links (although inevitably a few are broken) is http://members.aol.com/dheitm8612/page2.htm.

www.elknet.pl/acestory/aces.htm is a Polish site devoted to air aces from all the major air forces.

www.geocities.com/capecanaveral/runway/9601 contains transcripts of interviews with aircrew of all nations, but with a heavy American bias. Interesting all the same.

www.ww2aircraft.net is a web forum dedicated to the history of military aviation (especially for the Second World War). If you want a debate about which were the best and worst planes of the war, this is the place for you.

Even after over 50 years one of the best introductions to the history and achievements of the RAF during the war remains the official history of the RAF. The first volume, *The Fight at Odds* by Dennis Barker, was published in 1953 and covered the period roughly up to the end of 1941. It can be read at www.ibiblio.org/hyperwar/UN/UK/UK-RAF-I/index.html#contents.

A very detailed set of abbreviations used by the RAF during the war is at www.worldwar2exraf.co.uk/acronyms%20A.htm. They turn up with surprising frequency in documents and service records.

www.perth.igs.net/%7Elong/page3.htm#crewsanch contains various pages devoted to the war in the air, and includes a glossary of RAF slang (some of which may not be suitable for readers of a nervous disposition).

Ronald Quirk's pages at www.rquirk.com/index.html are very much a miscellanea containing material of interest to the webmaster. The site's strength lies in first-hand accounts, personal memoirs and detailed information on particular squadrons.

www.btinternet.com/~aquila/aviation.htm is a miscellaneous site on aviation and RAF history in the Isles of Scilly, Lincolnshire and Norfolk. The webmaster also runs tours around the 'Bomber Country' of East Anglia.

Organisational Structure And Commands

The structure of the RAF remained largely unchanged during the Second World War, being divided into a number of home commands, including Bomber, Coastal, Fighter and Maintenance, whose functions were obvious, plus a number of overseas commands arranged by theatre of operation, such as Middle Eastern Air Force (MEAF) and 2nd Tactical Air Force (which operated in North West Europe in 1944 and 1945). The best of known was Bomber Command, which has a number of websites. Curiously, there appear to be no websites devoted to other commands or overseas air forces.

www.rafcommands.com is a useful resource, providing details of the organisation of Bomber, Fighter and Coastal Commands, plus brief details of units attached to them. It duplicates, to an extent, the information found at www.rafweb.org/Menu.htm, which provides a detailed account of RAF organisation since 1918.

www.hellzapoppin.demon.co.uk is the site of the Bomber Command Historical Society. There are lots of interesting pages, although it is difficult to work out whether the site was redesigned in 2003 – as the home page still promises – or indeed, whether the Society is still in existence.

www.elsham.pwp.blueyonder.co.uk/raf_bc offers a superb introduction to Bomber Command and the men who served in it. The webmaster also maintains a losses database, recording the loss of bombers during the war and their crew members. Bob Baxter's similar, although better designed website, can be found at www.bomber-command.info.

Disappointingly, the Coastal Command and Maritime Air Association's website www.ccmaa.org.uk is mostly about the Association and its work. Of more interest – although, as the webmaster admits, frustratingly incomplete – is http://chat.carleton.ca/~jnoakes/ram/cc/index.html, which has a selection of orders of battle and the tactical instruction issued to aircrews on how to sink enemy submarines.

http://freespace.virgin.net/richard.wordsmith/roc/rochist.htm is a comprehensive site about the Royal Observer Corps between 1925 and 1992, when it was axed. Another useful site is provided by the Truro Branch of the ROC Association at www.truroroca.co.uk. The national Association itself can be found at www.rocassoc.org.uk.

Aircraft

The RAF flew a large number of different types of aircraft during the war. There are glossaries and databases of the aircraft in service with the world's air forces (see Chapter 7), but the websites here relate to specific types of machine. The British Aviation Resource Centre at www.warbirdsresourcegroup.org/BARC/index.html provides general information about British aircraft that saw service with the RAF. It is part of a larger site devoted to Second World War aircraft worldwide. In addition:

http://myweb.tiscali.co.uk/aeroplans/index.html offers construction plans for some British military and civil aircraft, originally built roughly between 1908 and 1945.

A major reference site about the flying boat, with a particular emphasis on material for modellers, can be found at www.seawings.co.uk. It includes details of flying boats worldwide.

http://mysite.orange.co.uk/aircraftwreckage/index.html contains photographs of the excavation of a 98 Squadron Fairey Battle from an Icelandic glacier in 2001.

www.myring.org.uk/beau is a detailed site devoted to the twin-engine Bristol Beaufighter.

The Blenheim Society is rebuilding a Bristol Blenheim at Duxford airfield. Find out more at www.blenheimsociety.org.uk.

The Catalina Society is devoted to the American Curtis Catalina flying boat, which saw service with the RAF during the war. More information is available at www.catalina.org.uk.

www.users.waitrose.com/~mbcass is devoted to Short 'C' class Empire flying boats. You can download construction plans, plus a copy of a book published by the webmaster on the aircraft.

http://surfcity.kund.dalnet.se looks at biplanes that saw service in the Second World War, including the Gloster Gladiators, which defended Malta in the dark days of 1941 and 1942. Another site about the Gloster Gladiator is www.geocities.com/acrawford0/index.html, with pages about machines operated by the Chinese Air Force.

According to www3.ns.sympatico.ca/hurricane/index.htm, the Hawker Hurricane 'destroyed more enemy aircraft during the World War II than all other aircraft combined. It was more manoeuvrable, a steadier gun platform, and could take more punishment.' There are some interesting pages including material about the Sea Hurricane. Meanwhile, the Cambridge

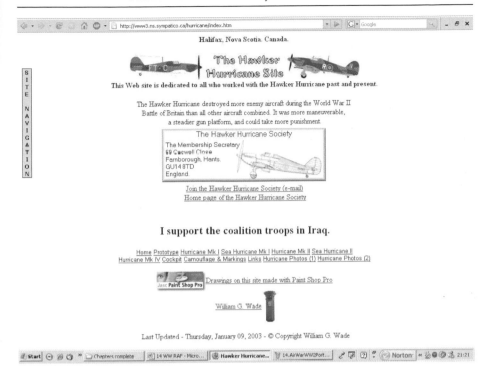

 http://www3.ns.sympatico.ca/hurricane/index.htm — Google

Halifax, Nova Scotia. Canada.

The Hawker Hurricane Site

This Web site is dedicated to all who worked with the Hawker Hurricane past and present.

The Hawker Hurricane destroyed more enemy aircraft during the World War II Battle of Britain than all other aircraft combined. It was more maneuverable, a steadier gun platform, and could take more punishment.

The Hawker Hurricane Society

The Membership Secretary
69 Caswell Close
Farnborough, Hants.
GU14 8TD
England.

Join the Hawker Hurricane Society (e-mail)
Home page of the Hawker Hurricane Society

I support the coalition troops in Iraq.

Home Prototype Hurricane Mk I Sea Hurricane Mk I Hurricane Mk II Sea Hurricane II
Hurricane Mk IV Cockpit Camouflage & Markings Links Hurricane Photos (1) Hurricane Photos (2)

Jasc Paint Shop Pro   Drawings on this site made with Paint Shop Pro

William G. Wade

Last Updated - Thursday, January 09, 2003 - © Copyright William G. Wade

Start | Chapters complete | 14 WW RAF - Micro... | Hawker Hurricane... | 14.AirWarWW2Port... | Norton | 21:21

Bomber and Fighter Society at www.cbfs.org.uk is restoring a Hawker Hurricane, which should fly in 2008.

www.lancaster-archive.com is a comprehensive site devoted to the Avro Lancaster bomber and its predecessor, the Manchester. The site works best with Internet Explorer. Another enthusiast's site can be found at http://website.lineone.net/~norman.groom, describing the construction of the Pilot's, Navigator's and Radio Operator's section of an Avro Lancaster, which can now be seen at Pitstone Green Museum on the Bedfordshire/Buckinghamshire borders. And if you want to see one in flight there is a short video clip at www.mikekemble.com/ww2/lanc.html, as well as a short history of the aircraft.

The all-wooden Mosquito was a gem of a reconnaissance aircraft. A couple of excellent websites about the aircraft are at www.home.gil.com.au/~bfillery/mossie.htm and http://mossie.org/Mosquito.html.

The North American P-51 Mustang was one of the great fighters used by the RAF from 1943 onwards. An unfortunately hard to read page about the aircraft is at http://www.icon.co.za/~pauljnr/history.htm.

Aviation historian John 'Dinger' Dell has a number of pages devoted to RAF aircraft of the Second World War at http://freespace.virgin.net/john.dell/index.htm, but it is mainly about the Blackburn Skua, which was a fighter/dive-bomber used by the Fleet Air Arm. A slightly strange Norwegian site about a Skua shot down on 27 April 1940 can be found at http://home.online.no/~oela.

www.deltaweb.co.uk/spitfire/index.htm provides a detailed history of the Supermarine Spitfire. Two other general sites about Spitfires are www.mikekemble.com/ww2/spitfire.html and www.angelfire.com/hi5/spitfiremk2a. The latter site tells the story of Spitfire Mk IIA P8144 'City of St Albans'. If you need more information, why not join the Spitfire Society at www.spitfiresociety.demon.co.uk.

Dilip Sarkar is an expert author on the Spitfire (and RAF and RN in the Second World War) and has an interesting, if rather self-congratulatory, site at www.dilipsarkarmbe.co.uk.

www.airwaveyachts.com.au/Aircraft/Index.html has lots of information about the Short Empire and Short Sunderland flying boats. There's a great video clip of a plane taking off, showing its power.

www.stirlingproject.co.uk is an interesting site devoted to a project to rebuild the front section of a Short Stirling bomber. Surprisingly, no aircraft or detailed plans survive. A more conventional history of the aircraft can be found at www.stirling.box.nl/home.htm. There are links to other sites of interest to Stirling enthusiasts.

www.perth.igs.net/%7Elong/wellington.htm contains pages devoted to the twin-engine Wellington bomber, familiarly known as 'the Wimpey' to crews.

Air Operations

www.lostbombers.co.uk is a superb resource, providing a database of bombers shot down with details of raids and crew members. It is also attractively presented. Of a more specialist nature is www.a1.nl/nfla/lijst.html, which contains a list of RAF and Allied planes that crashed over the Netherlands during the war and subsequently recovered. You need to click on the 'open lijst' button at the bottom, which opens a PDF document in English.

The Dambusters Raid took place on the night of 16 May 1943 and was one of the most famous exploits in the history of the RAF, although the raid did not actually achieve all of its objectives. The story is told at. www.dambusters.org.uk.

The project to put all aerial photos taken by the RAF and held by the Aerial Reconnaissance Archives at Keel University online seems to have been stillborn, but the website at www.evidenceincamera.co.uk contains some interesting sets of photographs, such as those concerning the D-Day landings.

www.airmuseum.ca is a Canadian site devoted to the British Commonwealth Air Training Plan, which trained thousands of RAF aircrew in Canada, Australia, Rhodesia and the USA.

A website still being built is www.acseac.co.uk/index.php, which is dedicated to the Liberator squadrons of the RAF and Commonwealth squadrons in South East Asia, with brief descriptions of individual aircraft. Another site on the subject is at www.rquirk.com, where there are several memoirs of pilots who flew the Liberator.

Battle of Britain

As might be expected, the Battle of Britain Historical Society website, www.battleofbritain.net, has lots about the battle, including a number of pages for students and a discussion board.

www.raf.mod.uk/bob1940/bobhome.html is the RAF's own comprehensive site, with details of the squadrons and stations that took part, and a roll of honour for the men who did not survive.

www.battle-of-britain.com is a comprehensive and attractive site devoted to the battle, and you can download a free screensaver. Another superb site is www.the-battle-of-britain.co.uk, which includes some biographies of 'the few'. And if you want to know why the battle had to be won, read the scary speech of Reichsminister Richard Darré reprinted here.

The Kent Battle of Britain Museum preserves the old station at RAF Hawkinge near Folkestone, which was the closest RAF airfield to France. Find out more at www.kbobm.org.

www.bbmf.co.uk/index.html is about the Battle of Britain Memorial Flight, which is the RAF's own collection of preserved aircraft from the period. If you want to book the Flight you can do so here.

Squadrons And Units

Many individual squadrons (and far fewer units) have websites devoted to them, but vary in quality. Although the emphasis is on the Second World War, there are often pages on pre- and post-war history.

www.rafmarham.co.uk/organisation/2squadron/2squadron.htm is the official website for 2 Squadron. According to the website, since its formation in 1912, its many achievements include the first use of airborne cameras in 1914, winning the first air Victoria Cross in 1915, and taking the first pictures of the D-Day landings in 1944.

Although mainly a reunion association for 6 Squadron, http://fly.to/sixsqnasso contains a number of pages about the squadron's history, which was formed in 1914, and is the longest continuously serving squadron in the RAF.

http://8squadron.co.uk/index.php is really a site about the modern RAF squadron, but there are some pages covering its history.

www.25squadron.org.uk is the website of the 25 Squadron Association, with a few pages on the unit's history.

An excellent squadron history for 41 Squadron is at http://brew.clients.ch/RAF41Sqdn.htm. It was a fighter squadron and there are biographies of over 320 pilots, including 64 who were killed in action and another 21 who were shot down and became prisoners of war.

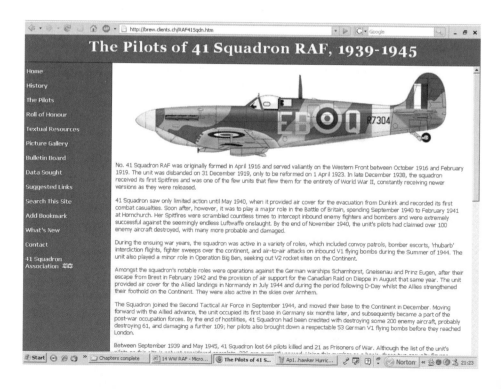

www.46squadron.info is the website for the 46 Squadron Association. There are some pages devoted to the squadron's history.

51 Squadron was a Halifax squadron within Bomber Command. Its story is told at www.geocities.com/pentagon/base/4213, although it is not comprehensive and gives the impression of having not been updated for a while.

The story of 74 Squadron appears at http://members.tripod.com/~dptidy/74sqna.html. It was a fighter squadron until disbanded in 2000 and had strong links with South Africa.

The website of 77 RAF Squadron Association at http://homepage.ntlworld.com/r_m_g.varley/77%20Squadron%20Associati on.htm contains a number of interesting pages about the squadron's wartime career.

It's not often that ground crew are commemorated in squadron histories or websites, which is why www.cs.kent.ac.uk/people/staff/djb/92squadron is particularly welcome, looking at the 'oiks' of 92 Squadron who kept the planes in good condition.

www.surfmydot.com/96squadron/index.htm is for 96 Squadron, although it is rather more a veterans' association than a site devoted to the squadron's history.

http://mainly99.users.btopenworld.com provides a history of 99 Squadron, which served mainly in South East Asia during the war.

www.100squadronassociation.org.uk is mainly an old comrades' association, but there are several pages about the squadron's history. So far, the history has reached up to 1922. Another site about the squadron can be found at www.angelfire.com/id/100sqn.

http://elshamwolds.50g.com is dedicated to 103 Squadron (and 576 Squadron, which was an offshoot), both bomber squadrons flying from Elsham Wolds during 1943 and 1944.

112 Squadron had a varied history during the war, serving in Greece, the Middle East and Italy. The squadron's story is well told at www.geocities.com/raf_112_sqdn.

A comprehensive site devoted to 150 Squadron's wartime exploits can be found at www.perth.igs.net/%7Elong/indexold.htm. Unfortunately, moving between pages can be very slow.

www.hillhead99.freeserve.co.uk is a comprehensive site devoted to 201 Squadron, including post-war material.

www.202-sqn-assoc.co.uk is for the 202 Squadron Association: there's not much on the history, although there are some nice stories by former members.

www.207squadron.rafinfo.org.uk is mainly a focus for 207 Squadron reunions, but there are a number of pages on its history, plus links to other interesting sites.

http://users.cyberone.com.au/clardo is a comprehensive site devoted to 211 Squadron, which served in the Middle East and the Far East. Another site, which includes many photographs taken from an album compiled by Geoffrey Grierson, a wartime member of the squadron, are at http://freespace.virgin.net/mike.grierson/211Sqn.

218 (Gold Coast) Squadron was a Bomber Command squadron flying Wellingtons and Stirlings. In 1943 623 Squadron was formed from it. More can be found at www.goldcoastsquadron218.co.uk/index.htm.

www.geocities.com/Athens/Agora/9349/index.htm is a detailed site about 221 Squadron, which flew Wellingtons during the war. There are some nice photographs and stories about missions.

www.250-squadron.freeserve.co.uk/pages/mainframe.htm tells the story of 250 (Sudan) Squadron, which was formed in 1941 and disbanded in 1947, having served as air support for the British Army in the Middle East and Italy.

609 Squadron was a fighter squadron and www.609wrsquadron.co.uk gives a real feeling for life in the Squadron. The page about the regimental mascot is well worth reading. Another site with photographs of the squadron taken by a member, Jack Lister, between 1937 and 1943, is at www.vord.net/609/index.htm.

www.624squadron.org is an impressive site devoted to 624 (Special Duties) Squadron, which flew in Italy. To navigate through the site you need to click on the bar at the top of the screen.

http://homepage.virgin.net/dave.stapleton9/index.htm is a very detailed site about 626 Squadron, which was formed in November 1943 within Bomber Command. It's most famous member was the comedian and writer Michael Bentine, who was an intelligence officer with the squadron (and there is a page about him).

www.644squadron.com tells the story of 644 Squadron, a special duties unit that served in Italy.

www.656squadron.org is an attractive site about 656 (Air Observation) Squadron which served in Burma. You might want to skip the Flash introduction however.

Pages about 19OTU and RAF Forres can be found at www.griffon.clara.net/19/master.htm. The site is difficult to navigate around.

RAF Stations

Some 600 airfields were rapidly built in the months leading up to the outbreak of war and during the war itself, across most of Britain, particularly East Anglia and the South East. Many would subsequently be passed over to the USAAF or Commonwealth squadrons. Inevitably, most were abandoned at the end of the war or during the slow decline in the size of the post-war RAF. There are a number of charities and other bodies seeking to protect or restore them. The Airfields of Britain Conservation Trust, for example, aims to preserve and protect our priceless airfields, and also to promote awareness of the historical heritage associated with them. More can be found at www.abct.org.uk.

More concerned with researching the history of airfields is the Airfield Research Group at www.airfield-research-group.co.uk. The site has many useful pages and book reviews.

http://worldwar2airfields.fotopic.net is an unusual site containing photographs of Second World War airfields, radar bases and other military installations, showing them as they are today.

Of a more specialist nature is www.controltowers.co.uk/Intro.htm, devoted to the study of airfields in the UK, particularly control towers or watch offices, which, as the site points out, constituted the heart of a station. There are some photographs.

Some individual stations or groups of neighbouring airfields also have sites. For example, modern photographs and descriptions of former RAF stations at King's Cliffe, Deenethorpe, Polebrook, Glatton and Kimbolton, all in Bedfordshire, can be found at www.fieldsofvalour.co.uk.

Pages about RAF Boxted, which housed a variety of USAAF units, can be found at www.boxted-airfield.com/index.htm.

www.burtonwoodbase.org is an interesting site about RAF Burtonwood, which opened in 1939 and is still in use. It was largely a USAAF base. There's even a page about the ghosts to be found there.

Despite the URL http://wartime-airfields.com is mainly about the small RAF stations near Harlow, Essex.

http://hunsdonmemorial.tripod.com tells the story of the memorial at RAF Hunsdon, which was dedicated in 2005.

www.raf-lichfield.co.uk is an impressive site devoted to the men and women who served at RAF Lichfield, which housed 51 MU and 27 OTU.

www.mhas.org.uk is the website for the preservation society and small museum devoted to RAF Martlesham Heath, on the edge of Ipswich, which opened in 1917 and closed in 1963. There are some interesting pages.

The RAF School of Technical Training at RAF Melksham between 1940 and 1964 is commemorated at www.ten-forward.demon.co.uk/melksham. There are some nice memories posted by men who served there.

www.wellingtonaviation.org/history/docs/index.htm is the website for a small museum dedicated to RAF Morton-in-the-Marsh, which housed 21 OTU. There is an interesting diary, which gives an idea of the sort of things that happened on a typical RAF base.

The story of RAF Nuthampstead, which housed several USAAF units, is told at www.station131.co.uk/Site%20Frame.htm.

One of the more unusual RAF stations was at Oban, on the edge of Highlands. It is where a number of flying boat squadrons were based during the war. More can be found at www.rafoban.co.uk. There are also pages about the death of the Duke of Gloucester in August 1942.

Pages about the new memorial at RAF Sawbridgeworth are at http://sawbomemorial.tripod.com.

RAF Tarrant Rushton was the point of departure for many wartime special operations in Europe. The website, www.tarrant-rushton.ndirect.co.uk/introduction.htm, contains then and now photographs and extracts from the station's operation record books (Form 540). Navigation between pages is rather slow.

The rather incomplete http://freespace.virgin.net/anne.welch/newpage11.htm has pages on Thorpe Abbots, the barely recognisable ruined tower at Metheringham and the 'Control Tower Cafe' at Westhampnett, a hanger at West Malling (used for the closing sequence of The Beatles film,

Magical Mystery Tour) and the wall paintings in the barrack blocks at Seething.

www.rafwmm.flyer.co.uk looks at RAF Wickenby in Lincolnshire, which was built in 1942 and closed in 1945, and housed 12 and 626 Squadrons. There is now a small museum.

The Experiences of Individual Airmen

There are a number of sites about the experiences of individuals and aircrew that give a flavour of what life must have been like. On the website for 150 Squadron, for example, there is a quote from Air Commodore H I Cozens, recalling his time flying Wellingtons in 1943: 'Anyone whose sole experience of flying is confined to holiday jets has simply no idea of what it was like to fly in a wartime bomber: the numbing cold, with icy winds seeking out the chinks in one's clothing . . . the shattering noise, the constant teeth jarring vibration, the turbulence causing the whole airframe to flex and creak; having to wear an oxygen mask which made every breath reek of wet rubber; the cramp which the tight harness made it impossible to relieve . . . '

Short biographies of a number of RAF and FAA pilots can be found at www.warbirdsresourcegroup.org/BARC/index.html, but it is by no means comprehensive.

http://home.westman.wave.ca/~hillmans/campbell.html is a Canadian site devoted to F/Lt William Gavin Campbell and the crew of Lancaster KB879, which crashed at Sandon, Staffs on 30 April 1945.

www.constable.ca/edwards.htm is the story, told in a curious third person style, of a Canadian pilot, James F 'Stocky' Edwards, who was a fighter pilot in 94 and 260 squadrons. There are some interesting observations about the state of training and on the enemy.

A site at www.lancastered627.bravehost.com is dedicated to rear gunner Flight Sergeant John Godwin and his fellow crew members of Lancaster ED627 of 207 Squadron, which was shot down over Germany in August 1943.

http://members.tripod.com/~jkoplitz/index.htm is devoted to John Francis Koplitz, an American who served with the RCAF and RAF in the Second World War.

Pilot Officer A G Lewis was shot down over France in 1940. http://homepages.tesco.net/~mrogers/CBFS/lastofthefew.html is about to him and his fellow pilots of 85 Squadron.

www.19clarendondrive.freeserve.co.uk is dedicated to the memory of Percy Milnes and the crew of Wellington bomber Z1206.F of 142 Squadron, who were killed in action over Germany in July 1942.

This site www.holum.net/gen/rafpilot.htm is about two brothers, Angus and Dougal Murray, who served as pilots in the RAF Voluntary Reserve.

The personal illustrated memoir of Wing Commander Geoffrey Hall 'Pop' Porter, who served in the RAF during and after the war, as well as in the pre-war Imperial Airways, can be found at www.trasksdad.com/PopsProgress.

Ron Roberts served with 3232 SCU (Servicing Commando Unit), which serviced aircraft as near as possible to the front line. His story, and more about the unit, is told at www.alliedspecialforces.org/royalairforceservicingcommandosrecollectionsronroberts3232page1.htm.

Some moving pages about Tommy Simpson, a wireless operator/air gunner with 101 Squadron, are at www.geocities.com/squarebasher2001/tribute.html.

http://myweb.tiscali.co.uk/janemarshallworld/TweedalesWarPages%201–35.htm offers an excellent autobiography of Henry Tweedale, from Rochdale, who became a wireless operator in 232 Squadron. The website's navigation leaves a lot to be desired and frustratingly the memoir stops just as he was captured by the Japanese in early 1942.

Douglas Webb served in 617 Squadron and took part in the Dambusters Raid. After the war he became a photographer. There is a page about his career at www.pamela-green.com/dambuster.live, which is a site largely devoted to Pamela Green, who was a pin-up model and actress of the 1950s (and later Mrs Douglas Webb).

Chapter 14

SECOND WORLD WAR – THE HOME FRONT

The Second World War saw the labour and life of every man, woman and child directed towards the cause of victory. Men and women over eighteen were conscripted into the forces or directed to work in factories, on the land or down the mines. Young and old alike had to survive on small rations of dull food. Despite the inevitable grumbling, this was a remarkably successful process.

Not all men went into the services: because of shortages of labour, 10 per cent of 18- and 19-year-old conscripts were directed down the mines from 1943. Known as Bevin Boys, after the Minister of Labour, the story of one of them is told at Bevin Boys: www.ewell-probus.org.uk/archive/bevin.htm. Women, too, played a full role in the war effort, which is described at http://caber.open.ac.uk/schools/stanway/index.html.

A civil defence network was set up, which included bodies such as the Home Guard (see below), Air Raid Precautions and the Women's Voluntary Service. An introduction can be found at http://wearcam.org/decon/cleansing_stations_civildefense.html#cdf.

And of course, many families were directly affected by the war. Nearly 61,000 civilians lost their lives as the result of enemy air action, while hundreds of thousands more were rendered homeless. Rolls of Honour for those who died in air raids can be found at www.cwgc.org.

In truth, civilians at home contributed as much to victory as the aircrew over Germany or soldiers in the jungles of Burma. A number of stories of men and women are available on the BBC's People's History website at www.bbc.co.uk/ww2peopleswar. There are some fascinating stories to be found there.

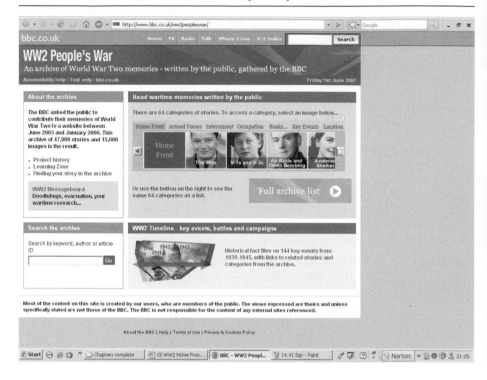

The Home Front is one of the key subjects studied in schools as part of the history syllabus part of the National Curriculum. As a result, there are a number of sites designed with schoolchildren very much in mind. Even so, on occasion they can be useful and simple introductions to what can be a complex subject. The National Archives' learning curve exhibition at www.learningcurve.gov.uk/homefront/default.htm, for example, is designed specifically for Key Stage 2 and 3. Sainsbury's supermarket has some interesting pages about shopping during the war at www.j-sainsbury.co.uk/museum/war_intro.htm.

One unusual civilian unit was the Air Transport Auxiliary (ATA), which was comprised of civilian pilots (including a number of women) who ferried aircraft from factories to the military airfields, where they were needed. The story of the American women pilots is told at www.airtransportaux.org with a more general history at www.fleetairarmarchive.net/RollofHonour/ATA/ATA.html.

www.homesweethomefront.co.uk/templates/hshf_frameset_tem.htm and www.historylearningsite.co.uk/homefront.htm are two other sites designed for older students. Of particular interest is an introduction to the Home Guard. Somewhat more advanced is http://myweb.tiscali.co.uk/

homefront/mwindex.html, which offers an introduction to the role of civil defence during the war.

Preparations For A German Invasion And The Home Guard

Of course the Germans never invaded. Nevertheless . . .

www.parhamairfieldmuseum.co.uk/brohome.html is the website of the British Resistance Museum with lots of pages devoted to the resistance planned had the Germans landed. At the heart of the resistance would have been a network of Auxiliary Units of the Home Guard, whose story is even today little known. A website devoted to them and their activities are at www.auxunit.org.uk, with additional material at www.warlinks.com/pages/auxiliary.html.

An analysis of Operation SEELÖWE (SEALION), the German invasion plan, and why it would have failed, can be found at www.flin.demon.co.uk/althist/seal1.htm.

www.pillboxesuk.co.uk is an interesting site about the 6,000 (out of 65,000) remaining pillbox defences that were hurriedly built during the summer of 1940 as strongpoints in case of invasion. There are also links to sites about pillboxes in Somerset and Hertfordshire.

At the forefront of any resistance would have been the Home Guard (forever immortalised in the BBC TV series as 'Dad's Army'), comprised of volunteers hurriedly formed in the summer of 1940. Its history is told at www.home-guard.org.uk and there are links to the Chatham Home Guard – a re-enactment unit. Another group of re-enactors is the Victory in Europe Re-enactment Association (VERA) at www.vera.org.uk/HGMINISITECONTENTS.htm, with pages about the uniforms worn by the men.

The story of Aldridge Home Guard is told at www.staffshomeguard.co.uk. The site is based on a history of the unit produced in 1945. But there is much more than that, with many pages about the Home Guard in general, as well as links to other relevant sites. A page about Ray South's experiences in the Windsor Home Guard is at www.thamesweb.co.uk/windsor/windsorhistory/homeguard.html.

A facsimile of a Home Guard training booklet can be found at http://met.open.ac.uk/group/jwL/hg_manual/01.htm. And, lastly, if you are interested in the fictional Dad's Army, then the Whispers from Walmington site at www.davecovcomedy.co.uk/whispersfromwalmington/index.htm is a good place to start.

The War Locally

Of course, the war affected local communities and local people in many different ways. There are still enough people alive to remember life then, and their memories add a lift to a number of these sites.

A county wide site for Bedfordshire can be found at www.galaxy.bedfordshire.gov.uk/webingres/bedfordshire/vlib/0.digitised_resources/digitisation_wwii.htm, which has links to research on Bedfordshire, with pages about RAF bases, the Home Guard and memories of local people both civilian and military. The highlight is probably a database of members of the Women's Land Army in the county.

www.bbc.co.uk/northernireland/yourplaceandmine/topics/war/belfastblitz/ tells the story of German air attacks on Belfast. Undoubtedly one of the best sites about the Home Front is www.brandonatwar.co.uk, which tells the story of Brandon, a small market town in Suffolk, with memories of local people and a day by day diary.

The heaviest air raids took place over Clydebank, near Glasgow, when on 13 and 14 March 1941, the *Luftwaffe* executed a brutal attack on the town, dealing a devastating blow from which the area never fully recovered. Details can be found at http://theclydebankstory.com/story_TCSB01.php.

www.familyresearcher.co.uk has details of the people who were killed in raids on Coventry, including, of course, the famous raid of 14 November 1940. There are also pages on the Home Guard and other aspects of life in the city.

Long known as the 'lock and key of the Kingdom', Dover had an exciting war, which is told at www.dover-kent.co.uk/history/world_war_2.htm. There are also pages on the First World War.

In West Cumberland, Holmbroook Hall was taken over by the Navy as HMS *Volcano*, which is where men were trained for bomb disposal work. Its story

and that of the men who were there is told at www.users.globalnet.co.uk/ ~rwbarnes/defence/volcano.htm.

www.dalbeattie.com/ministryofsupplyfactorydalbeattie/rollofhonour.htm offers a history of the Cordite Factory at Dalbeattie near Moffat, South West Scotland, which employed over 3,000 civilians, more than two-thirds of whom were women. The intention is to provide a roll of honour. There should be more sites like this, because it is hard to find anything about the men and women who worked in munitions factories during either world war.

Eastbourne experienced 93 air raids between July 1940 and August 1940. They are briefly described at www.btinternet.com/~williamenigma/eb2ww0.htm. Unfortunately, the site appears to be incomplete.

The Living Memory Association has been collecting wartime memories of people in Edinburgh, many of which are shared at www.livingmemory.org.uk/index.html. They include a number of audio clips.

www.bpears.org.uk/NE-Diary offers a day by day account of events along the coast between Hull and Berwick-upon-Tweed. It is mainly about military activities such as air attacks on ships or raids on coastal areas.

Although primarily about contaminated land www.contaminatedland.co.uk/sere-dip/estd-uxb.htm#BREADCRUMBS contains a list of unexploded bombs still to be found in the London area.

http://mysite.wanadoo-members.co.uk/wartime_orkney/index.jhtml contains pages about the fortifications and the former RAF and naval bases on the Orkney islands.

www.slaidburn.org.uk/ww2.htm tells the story of the small Lancashire village of Slaidburn, with pages about the Home Guard, evacuees and agricultural production. There's also a roll of honour for men who did not return.

Miscellaneous Sites

Ciphers and codes played a big role in the Allied victory, a detailed site about the equipment used and how the codes were broken is at www.codesandciphers.org.uk. Code-breaking largely took place at Bletchley Park, now a museum devoted to codes and computers on the edge of Milton Keynes, with a website at www.bletchleypark.org.uk. One can buy a pocket Enigma machine from their on-line bookshop.

The greatest of the cryptographers was Alan Turing. Many of his papers are now available online at www.turing.org.uk/turing/scrapbook/ww2.htm. Another leader was Sir Harry Hinsley: notes of a lecture he gave back in 1993 in Cambridge are at www.cl.cam.ac.uk/research/security/Historical/hinsley.html. www.tarrif.net contains a database of Allied and Axis military equipment, with specifications of each item. The site is really an adjunct to the *Battleground Europe* computer simulation game.

www.qsl.net/pe1ngz/signalscollection.html is a slow to load but detailed Dutch site, looking at signalling within British and American forces.

A fun site is at www.cyber-heritage.co.uk/cutaway, which has wartime illustrations largely from children's magazines of the period explaining how anti-aircraft guns, submarines and the like worked.

Memories

The Second World War Experience Centre in Leeds maintains an archive and oral history centre. The website at www.war-experience.org has material about the Centre's work.

More impressive and comprehensive is the BBC's People's War project at www.bbc.co.uk/ww2peopleswar, which is recording the memories of the men and women who were alive during the period. Some 47,000 people responded and there are lots of their stories to be found here. A similar site is at www.wartimememories.co.uk.

www.britain-at-war.org.uk contains a number of accounts by individuals of their experiences in the war or biographies of fathers or grandfathers who were there. A nice idea is www.war-letters.com, which is a collection of transcribed letters written by British and American soldiers. Unfortunately, few letters are actually available. Another similar site is ww2.war-letters.com.

Photographs And Posters

There are a number of collections of photographs and posters of varying quality available online. Photographs relating to aviation are described elsewhere, but here are a few others:

The Second World War saw the greatest triumph of the poster as an art form. Most prominent artists of the period drew these posters, illuminating memorable campaigns such as 'dig for victory' and 'coughs and sneezes spread diseases'. www.ww2poster.co.uk provides a database of illustrators of many of the most famous British war posters, with illustrations of a number of posters themselves. Unfortunately, the type size is tiny and as a result the site can be hard to read.

Perhaps of more immediate appeal, the National Archives has an on-line exhibition The Art of War at www.nationalarchives.gov.uk/theartofwar, which showcases many of the posters and related drawings held by the Archives. Another site providing background information (designed for a university course) is at www.st-andrews.ac.uk/~pv/pv/courses/posters.

If you want to buy reproduction of these posters then www.postersofwar.co.uk is a good place to try, with an unrivalled selection of images from around the world.

www.movinghistory.ac.uk/homefront/index.html is a selection of fascinating short films and newsreels about life in the Second World War, now deposited at regional film archives. Most were taken by amateurs. A number are about the Home Guard and civil defence.

http://warphotos.basnetworks.net has a lot of images about equipment and pages for the Second World War and other conflicts. I like the page on railway guns.

A collection of colour photographs is available at www.ww2incolor.com/gallery/ww2incolor.

Another collection of miscellaneous photographs is http://worldwartwozone.com/photopost, although you have to register to view any image at a reasonable size.

The University of North Texas have digitised its collection of mainly American posters and handbills in a simple to use site at http://digital.library.unt.edu/search.tkl?type=collection&q=WWII

Links

There are several sites mainly consisting of links to other websites, so if, heaven forbid, you can't find what you want in this book, these may help:

www.salientpoints.com is a slightly disappointing site purporting to cover both wars. It has many useful links to other Second World War sites. Of more use is www.warlinks.com, which has links to hundreds of websites with a British emphasis.

ww2.klup.info is a Dutch portal with links to hundreds of sites worldwide. When I visited the most popular sites were devoted to German songs of the period, Russian military maps and Italian Army equipment.

http://vlib.iue.it/history/mil/ww2.html has hundreds of links covering all aspects of the war.

Chapter 15

POST-WAR CONFLICTS AND EXPERIENCES

It is well known that, with the exception of 1968, British servicemen have died on active service in every year since the end of the Second World War. In 1945 the immediate tasks of the armed services were to maintain preparedness for war with Russia, and to disengage from the Empire. Within three years of the defeat of Japan, Britain had left India and Palestine. In 1950 British troops helped defend South Korea against aggression from the Communist North, which was backed by China and the Soviets.

But perhaps the greatest change was the slow realisation that the United Kingdom was no longer a great power. Defence reviews in 1957 and 1967 made clear the need to cut our military commitments, particularly 'East of Suez' as the phrase went. The result has seen a gradual shrinkage in the size of the armed forces. Thus it became increasingly obvious that our future lay in Europe as a close ally of the United States through the North Atlantic Treaty Organisation (NATO). Indeed, when the Americans disapproved of British actions, as they did over the Suez Invasion of 1956, it was very clear that the British could no longer act as a truly independent nation.

From the late 1940s until the early 1990s the chief threat was perceived as coming from the Soviet Union, and a perilous stand-off, known as the Cold War, was maintained at great economic cost. The National Cold War Exhibition provided by the RAF Museum at RAF Cosford in Shropshire, tells the story. More can be found at www.nationalcoldwarexhibition.org.uk, although, as the site was clearly designed with the needs of the National Curriculum in mind, it is short on content.

Since the end of the Cold War in the early 1990s the role of the armed forces has changed, in many ways reverting to a model that might have been familiar 100 years or so ago: overstretched troops fighting small wars in faraway countries, often for uncertain reasons.

If you want to know more about the issues facing the armed forces today then www.modoracle.com is a good place to start. If you are more interested in facts and figures, then www.armedforces.co.uk/armyindex.htm (for the

British Army), www.armedforces.co.uk/navyindex.htm (Royal Navy) and www.armedforces.co.uk/armyindex.htm (RAF) may be more of use.

I've always been impressed by the commonsense views of Tim Garden when he appears on TV. He is a former RAF Air Marshal and now the Liberal Democrat's defence spokesman in the House of Lords. He maintains an interesting site at www.tgarden.demon.co.uk, where he occasionally blogs on defence issues of the day.

A more controversial site, which discusses the modern Royal Navy, is at http://navy-matters.beedall.com. Its conclusions make depressing reading, revealing years of Treasury penny-pinching and unimaginative planning. Perhaps the equivalent for the Army is the British Army Rumour Service at www.arrse.co.uk (there are equivalents for the Navy and RAF as well).

National Service

National Service between 1949 and 1963 brought hundreds of thousands of young men (willing or otherwise) into the services.

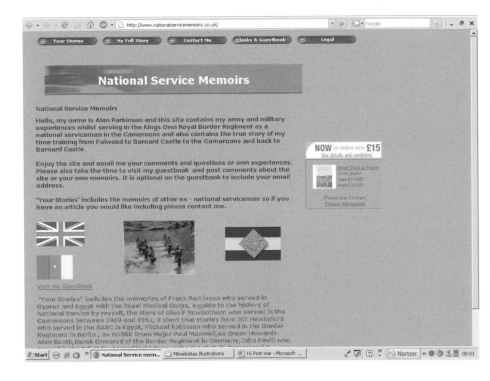

www.nationalservicememoirs.co.uk is an attractive site containing the reminiscences of Alan Parkinson, a National Serviceman with the King's Own Royal Border Regiment, who was based in North Yorkshire and, unusually, in the Cameroons, West Africa. There are also several other memoirs contributed by other former National Servicemen.

For the RAF, www.geocities.com/squarebasher2001 offers a superb nostalgic guide, with contributions from a number of former National Servicemen. There are a number of personal sites maintained by former National Servicemen, including Gerald Finlay, who was trained at RAF West Kirby and served at RAF Yatesbury and RAF Topcliffe (www.freewebs.com/themeadows/index.htm) and James Aitkin in Transport Command (www.freewebs.com/exrafairmovements/raflyneham.htm).

Post-1945 Conflicts

In many ways, if you studying post-war military history, you really only need visit one site: Britain's Small Wars – www.britains-smallwars.com – a superb and comprehensive site devoted to the various conflicts British forces have been engaged in since the Second World War, from India to Iraq. What

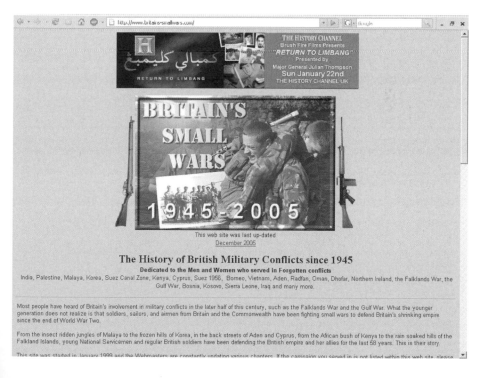

makes it so good are the contributions from the men who were there. If you are not sure, look at the discussion about the British 'involvement' in Vietnam. It is a serious, scholarly, and above all, sensible site. In my opinion it is one of the top ten websites for military history.

Korea

The Korean War was the first and largest conflict fought under the aegis of the United Nations, although it was overwhelmingly an American effort. It began in June 1950 when the Communist North Koreans invaded the South, and was concluded by an uneasy ceasefire signed in 1953, which is still in place. Britain was the third largest contributor of forces after the United States and South Korea, sending a number of infantry regiments and Royal Navy ships.

www.korean-war.com – an introductory site to the history of the Korean War. Although American, it does give due prominence to the contributions of other members of the United Nations, although the section for Britain is rather disappointing.

http://home.att.net/~C.C.Jordan/Korea.html – an American site devoted to the air war in Korea, although it does mention the British and Commonwealth air contributions in passing. There are links to other American sites with additional material.

http://assoc.orange.fr/france-coree/eurokorvet/uk/uk.htm – has links to veterans associations and various pages on the war. Another page, http://assoc.orange.fr/france-coree/eurokorvet/uk/ minewarfare_korea.htm, is a memoir of the Anglo-French naval involvement in the invasion of Inchon.

British losses during the Korean War (1950–1953) were 1109 killed and 2,674 wounded. Deaths are listed online at www.uk.or.kr/wargrave (with pictures of many of the graves).

www.remuseum.org.uk/corpshistory/rem_corps_part19.htm#korea contains a detailed description of the involvement of the Royal Engineers.

www.iwm.org.uk/upload/package/24/korea/koreaintro.htm is an on-line exhibition containing interviews with a few of the British and Commonwealth veterans of the Korean War.

www.chls11113.pwp.blueyonder.co.uk/ukvets/index.htm is the home page of the British Korean Veterans Association. It very much concerns itself with the Association's business rather than the history of the war.

Malaya and Borneo

The National Malaya and Borneo Veterans Association is for men and women (military and civilians) who were in the area during the Second World War and post-war years. Its website is www.nmbva.co.uk and contains some useful information, such as rolls of honour, mainly for British and Commonwealth civilians. The Association's Colchester branch also has a website, http://groups.msn.com/NMDistrictBranch/home.msnw, and has some useful links (although inevitably some are broken). www.ukmilitarygraves.org.my is a website dedicated to identifying and preserving British war graves (and those of civilians as well) in Malaysia.

The Australian site http://askari_mb.tripod.com provides an introduction to the Malayan Emergency. An interesting and (very long) webpage about the psychological warfare practised during the Emergency is at www.psywar.org/malaya.php.

Suez

It is hard to find much about the Suez Invasion of 1956, which was a botched attempt to stop Egypt's nationalisation of the Suez Canal. There are, however, two sites worth visiting. The first is www.suezveteransassociation.co.uk, which is the website of the Suez Veterans Association, with a list of members. Less relevant is www.suezcanalzone.com, an interesting site about the British forces that served in the Suez Canal Zone between 1950 and 1955, with a nice mixture of text and photographs, leavened with some humour.

The Falklands

The Falklands War took place between April and June 1982 as British forces defeated Argentine invaders, 8,000 miles from home. It was a remarkable, if controversial, achievement. There are a number of sites, some of which are linked to 25th Anniversary commemorations in 2007.

www.falklands25.com is the official site for the Falklands 25 Commemorative celebrations, but it is more use because it contains a summary of the campaign and a description of the Falkland Islands.

More about the 25th Anniversary celebrations with a timeline and a roll of honour of the men who lost their lives is at www.raf.mod.uk/falklands/index.html. There is also an impressive history of the conflict with lists of forces present and a virtual tour of the battlefields.

The National Army Museum has an on-line exhibition about the conflict at www.national-army-museum.ac.uk/exhibitions/Falklands.

www.sama82.org/index.htm is the website of the South Atlantic Medal Association, which is for veterans of the campaign.

www.falklandsmilitarylife.co.fk is an intriguing site designed to brief squaddies about life during their tours of duty on the Falklands today.

www.naval-history.net has a number of pages relating to naval aspects of the Falklands campaign. However, you will need to scroll almost to the bottom of the home page to find them. It is possible to download an e-book about the campaign by the webmaster.

www.hmsbrilliant.com is an explanation of the story of HMS *Brilliant* during the Falklands War by a member of the crew, with some interesting photographs.

www.iwm.org.uk/upload/package/3/falklands/falkintro.htm contains audio clips of interviews by the IWM Sound Archive, with some of the men who were there.

Royal Navy

The Experiences of Individual Seamen

For some reason there are a surprising number of websites devoted to webmasters' time in the Royal Navy. It seems to be a naval phenomenon, because there aren't many sites for the Army or the RAF. There are also sites devoted to a particular ship, which often include pages about crew members and memoirs of life on-board ship. Curiously, it is usually impossible to find the names of the webmasters, but presumably they, and the people they are writing for, know who they are.

www.witzend.pwp.blueyonder.co.uk/start.htm displays the home knit memoirs of a seemingly anonymous sailor (at least I couldn't find his name) on *Bulwark*, *Fearless*, *Antrim* and other ships in the 1960s and 1970s. Strange navigation and rather incomplete, but well worth visiting.

www.hmscavalier.org.uk is an excellent and comprehensive site about the destroyer HMS *Cavalier* between 1944 and 1972 with histories, crew lists and memoirs of those on board.

www.royalnavymemories.com – despite the URL, it is devoted to the post-war careers of HMS *Devonshire* and HMS *Leopard* and the webmaster's service on board them. One of my top ten weird sites. You'll have to visit to find out why!

www.burrill12.freeserve.co.uk/Contents.htm mainly consists of memories of service on-board HMS *Echo*, a coastal survey ship based at Chatham in the 1950s and 1960s. Strangely elegiac.

www.hmsgambia.com is a site maintained by the HMS *Gambia* Association, with lots about the commissions undertaken by the ship in the 1940s and 1950s.

http://brisray.com/index.html is a wonderful miscellany of a site. Included here because it has pages about the webmaster's father's career on-board HMS *Gambia* and HMS *Warrior* between 1950 and 1955, but there are also pages about the webmaster's career in the Territorial Army and, curiously, the various nasty illnesses he has had.

www.hms-juno.co.uk is a slightly strange site devoted to HMS *Juno* between 1970 and 1972, but with some nice stories and jokes. I recommend the one concerning bread and butter.

http://freespace.virgin.net/michael.overton1/hms.htm is fine site devoted to HMS *London* in the late 1940s, and the webmaster's father, David Overton's, service on board. There are also pages about the Yangtse Incident.

www.hmslondonderry.co.uk features a voyage on HMS *Londonderry* between 1960 and 1962. Mainly a reunion site for old shipmates, but there is a bit about the history of the ships that had the same name.

www.hmsplymouth.co.uk is home to the HMS *Plymouth* old comrades association. The ship served for thirty years between 1958 and 1988, including the Falklands War: indeed, the Argentine surrender was signed in the ship's wardroom. Photos of the ship (and links to a video on YouTube) are at www.pwsts.org.uk/hmsplymouth.

www.btinternet.com/~george.w.caton/index2.htm features the old comrades association for HMS *Unicorn*, largely for the period between 1947–1954. The webmaster's own site, www.george.w.caton.btinternet.co.uk/homepage.htm, is also worth visiting. He joined the RN as a naval cadet in 1948 and served on HMS *Unicorn*, HMS *Warrior* and submarines until retiring 1958. Worth reading, but the horrendous bright blue background is hard on the eyes.

web.ukonline.co.uk/macwarrior3/Home.html displays one man's memories of HMS *Terror*, the shore station in Singapore between 1961 and 1967.

www.hms-vanguard.co.uk shares Shirley North's memories of his voyage on HMS *Vanguard*, the last battleship in the early 1950s: excellent and evocative.

Royal Navy – Miscellaneous

www.hongkongflotillaassociation.co.uk is the website of the Hong Kong Flotilla Association for former members of motor boats, which operated in Hong Kong from the late 1940s. There are lots of useful photographs and plenty of information.

www.axfordsabode.org.uk/comishbk.htm contains a selection of unofficial commissioning books for a selection of post-war naval ships, full of valuable information about life onboard. They are downloaded in sections as PDFs, which take some time if you haven't got broadband. The site also has other pages devoted to naval life between the 1940s and 1980s.

www.mcdoa.org.uk is the website of the Minewarfare and Clearance Diving Officers Association. There are some nice stories and memories. I recommend the account of a trip to Aden in 1989.

Royal Air Force

Aircraft

One of the best general sites is www.vflintham.demon.co.ukm, which has brief histories of many of the aircraft flown by the RAF/FAA since the war. Frustratingly, however, links to many potentially interesting pages are broken. Covering much the same ground and visually more attractive is www.drivearchive.co.uk/xplanes.

There are a number of sites containing photographs of aircraft, some have many thousands of images available. Three of them are:

- http://myweb.tiscali.co.uk/ollieswebspace/index.htm

- www.milairpix.com

- www.paulnann.com

Many of these photographs were taken at air shows, which take place at airfields throughout the summer: www.airshows.co.uk has reviews of some of them (in small type which makes them hard to read) and links to the websites of forthcoming events.

There are a variety of sites devoted to individual aircraft types flown by the RAF since the war. Most were created by restoration societies or by individual enthusiasts. They include:

An ungainly but popular transport aircraft was the Blackburn Beverly, which flew with the RAF in the 1950s and 1960s. Pages about it can be found at beverley-association.org.uk.

www.buccsociety.com is the website of the Blackburn Buccaneer Society, dedicated to restoring a couple of aircraft at Buntingthorpe. Photographs of the aircraft can be found at http://ourworld.compuserve.com/homepages/andrewbrooks1/themight.htm.

A details devoted to the English Electric Canberra can be found at www.bywat.co.uk/canframes.html

http://website.lineone.net/~hunterxf382 is dedicated to Pete Buckingham's struggle to restore Hawker Hunter XF382 at the Midland Air Museum in Coventry (www.midlandairmuseum.co.uk). There are also some pages about RAF Bawdry in South Wales.

www.btinternet.com/~javelin features a history of the Gloster Javelin, the world's first delta winged, twin-engine fighter.

www.lightning.org.uk/home.html is a short history of the English Electric Lightning. The similarly named www.lightnings.org.uk is a Lightning Preservation Society based at Buntingthorpe, maintaining two of the last remaining aircraft. Of less interest is www.thunder-and-lightnings.co.uk, although it is one of a family of websites dedicated to British aircraft of the 1950s and 1960s. Meanwhile, www.lightningpilots.com contains a selection of photographs, arranged by squadron, of the aircraft and some of the pilots who flew them.

www.meteorflight.com looks at the Gloster Meteor, the RAF's first jet aircraft, introduced into service in the last months of the Second World War.

www.thegrowler.org.uk is the website of the Shackleton Association, dedicated to the memory of the Avro Shackleton and the men who flew the aircraft, primarily in its anti-submarine and maritime patrol roles.

www.tvoc.co.uk is the professional looking site of the Vulcan to the Sky Trust, which is attempting to restore Vulcan XH558 to flying order.

RAF Stations

The RAF maintain websites for many of its current stations, such as the one for RAF Valley at www.raf.mod.uk/rafvalley. Apart from this there are a number of sites devoted to current and former RAF airfields, which operated in the post-war period, including:

RAF Church Fenton in Yorkshire is one of an increasingly small number of operational airfields. It opened in 1937 and now houses the Yorkshire Universities Air Squadron and various other training units, although it began life as a fighter station.

RAF Gan, which was located on a desert island in the Maldives until it closed in 1976, has a number of sites compiled by people who saw service there, including http://hometown.aol.com/llerris/rafgan.html and especially www.gan.philliptsmall.me.uk and http://members.lycos.co.uk/ganisland (which offers trip to the island).

Another man at Gan was John Cooper. He has an interesting site at http://splashdown2.tripod.com about his service in the RAF in the Far East, the Handley Page Hastings in the 1950s and 1960s, and a mysterious crash he was involved in. It is strangely designed, so you will need to scroll down each page to find new material. John's photographs are posted at http://community.webshots.com/user/hastingsgan.

RAF Mauripur (No. 48 Staging Post) was located 10km north of Karachi and operated as a Royal Air Force base from 1943 until the formation of Pakistan, in 1947. However, the RAF still maintained its presence there until the end of

1956, sharing facilities with the Pakistan Air Force. It was the last active British unit on the Indian subcontinent. Its story is told at http://rafmauripur.org.uk.

www.drivearchive.co.uk/xplanes/valley.htm contains pages about RAF Valley in Anglesey, and provides a wide range of links to other websites.

It is also worth checking the sites of the various aviation museums (see Chapter 4) because they often include histories of the airfields they are based at. In addition, www.gan.philliptsmall.me.uk/00%20-%20HTML/RAFStations.htm includes a database of post-war RAF stations around the world, indicating where they were based.

The Experiences of Individual Airmen

As with the Navy, there are many sites containing memories or autobiographies of former RAF members, many of which are very evocative. Here is a selection:

www.freewebs.com/exrafenglish44–65 features Squadron Leader Jack Riley's career in the RAF in the Far East between 1944 and 1965, with some amusing stories and insights into an almost forgotten part of RAF history.

www.freewebs.com/roverjag is about Derek Lehrle's career at Chia Keng Radio Receiving Station in Singapore in the late 1950s.

www.bill-wood.co.uk is the autobiography of Bill Wood, who was in the first RAF Jet Aerobatic Team (precursor to the Red Arrows). He joined in 1942 and served for over twenty years.

www.104thlocking.org.uk is about the 104th training course for Aircraft Apprentices, No. 1 Radio School, RAF Locking, between May 1963 and April 1966, which trained 41 young men to be ground radar fitters. There are also pages on the RAF station itself, which closed in 1999. Another site for former apprentices concerns the 96th entry at RAF Halton between 1960 and 1963 at www.halton96th.co.uk and www.40thcosford.org.uk is for the 40th Boy Entrants at RAF Cosford in the 1960s, with lots of photographs.

Miscellaneous Sites

There are inevitably a number of sites that don't fit into the categories above, but are of interest. They include:

http://howitreallywas.typepad.com/ is a blog about the British occupation of Germany after the Second World War. It's not as dry as it sounds!

The National Archives has a number of public information films from 1945 to the 1980s on their website at www.nationalarchives.gov.uk/films. Some of these deal with military and defence matters.

In the early 1970s the American attempted to raise the Soviet nuclear submarine *K129*, which was lost in the Pacific in 1968, this is how they did it: http://mikekemble.pwp.blueyonder.co.uk/k129.html

The Vietnam War was one, of course, which the British missed out on. Even so, one Australian's experience of serving in South Vietnam in 1971 at www.david-pye.com/tourofduty71/index.php is worth exploring.

www.palacebarracksmemorialgarden.org is a Northern Irish on-line memorial to men and women from the province who lost their lives in the many post-war conflicts. Entries describe how the individuals died. The Gardens themselves are at Hollywood Barracks in County Down.

Still on Northern Ireland, www.sinnfein.org/bmgii/barmy.html provides a list of British Army facilities in the provinces over the past forty years. The site is maintained by Sinn Féin (the political arm of the IRA) so it is probably pretty accurate.

air-despatch.co.uk is the website about the Air Despatch Association, with something about their history. Judging by the photographs some serious drinking goes on at their reunions.

www.parachuteregiment-hsf.org is for and about the men who served with 5 Company, 10 Parachute Regiment, who were part of the Home Service Force, which was formed in 1983 to combat the threat from *Spetsnaz*, the Russian Special Forces (see www.spetsnaz-gru.com for details of hand-to-hand combat training). The site is surprisingly informative, but unfortunately, and irritatingly, as you move from page to page some bug insists in trying to send the webmaster an email.

http://mysite.wanadoo-members.co.uk/rafpa is the curious website of the RAF Police Association, with a mixture of Association matters and reminiscences about life in the RAF police.

http://mysite.wanadoo-members.co.uk/raf.police/index.jhtml consists mainly of personal photographs. The webmaster is trying to contact RAF dog handlers and RAF police based in the Suez Canal area and Hong Kong in the early 1950s. If you are interested in the American military's use of dogs www.olive-drab.com has a page on 'war dogs'.

www.ejectorseats.co.uk is devoted to the ejector seat, featuring different types, and how they were tested.

ww.spyflight.co.uk/main looks at the contentious issue of spy flights, mainly by the RAF and USAF, during the Cold War and after. It specialises in describing the aircraft used in the flights.

In the 1950s and 1960s the British had a programme to develop short and long-range missiles, either alone or with their European allies. The story of these endeavours (with descriptions of the missiles themselves) is told at www.spaceuk.org/index.htm.

www.faafieldgun.org is about the Fleet Air Arm (and RN) field gun crews who took part in the annual competition at the Royal Tournament between 1947 and 1999, which re-enacted the exploits of the Naval Brigade, which helped relieve Ladysmith by pulling guns and limbers across country from Durban, overcoming vast obstacles. This display was referred to as the toughest team event ever.

www.btinternet.com/~a.c.walton/navy/smn-faq/slang1.htm contains pages of jargon and terminology used in the Royal Navy and other English-speaking navies, some of it, it has to be said, is hardly usable in polite circles. It is part of a larger website on (mostly) American naval history.

Chapter 16

ENGLISH-SPEAKING ALLIES

First World War

The self-governing dominions – Australia, Canada, New Zealand and South Africa – each played a full part in the war effort. And in each case their experiences, particular of the poor quality of British military command and their tactics in wasting the lives of many thousands of young men, led to an emergence of local nationalism, best seen in the ANZAC Day celebrations in Australia and New Zealand, which commemorate the landings at Gallipoli on 21 April 1915.

Australia

Supposedly devoted to maintaining the spirit and memories Australian troops (often referred to as 'diggers'). www.diggerz.org/~anzacs/fffaif.htm is the website of the Friends and Families of the First Australian Imperial Force research institute and charity. There is a lot about the experiences of Diggers, wherever they served during the First World War. Unfortunately, it does not seem to have been updated for several years. Another site covering much the same subject is at www.ausmil.com/users/Anzacs.

Australia really came to nationhood during the ill-fated Gallipoli campaign of 1915, so it is not surprising that there are several excellent websites on the subject – www.anzacs.net has many pages about the battles themselves and the Australians who fell there. Meanwhile, www.anzacs.org has short biographies of the 492 ANZAC officers who died on the peninsula.

For the remainder of the war the Australians largely fought on the Western Front. www.diggertours.com is an excellent and well-designed site devoted to the men who lost their lives on the Western Front and their experiences there. There is a useful database describing the cemeteries where Aussies are buried, plus advice for people intending to visit the battlefields.

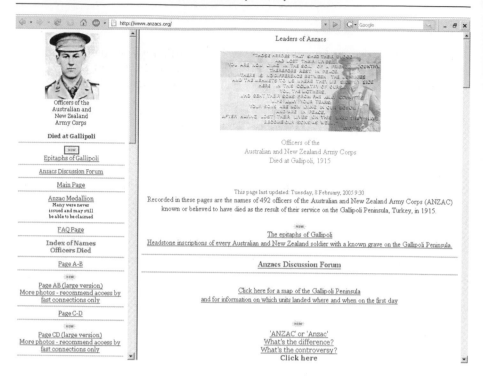

For many years Ross Bastian has been making beautiful bronze plaques and presenting them to places where the Australians fought in both world wars. More about his project can be found at www.plaques.satlink.com.au.

www.ciaops.com/guides/battle is an informative site about the battles in which the Australians were engaged in from 1916 onwards. Unfortunately, at the time of writing, the site appeared to be down. http://hamelfriends.free.fr/start.html is a strangely designed site but informative about the Battle of Hamel on 4 July 1918, in which 800 Australians were killed.

A number of diaries kept by the men who were there have been transcribed and placed online. They include those of Lt Ralph Doughty, MC, between April 1915 and March 1917, who was at Gallipoli and then in France, see www.thekivellfamily.co.nz/family_pages/ralphs_diaries/Ralph_Doughty.html. Pte Ernest George King also severed at Gallipoli and France and his diary is at http://users.bigpond.net.au/rhearne/index.htm.

www.nashos.org.au/15diary contains the diary of Cpl Ivor Alexander Williams, who was on the Western Front. However, he seems to have spent a lot of time in England at various theatrical performances.

Canada

The best place to find information about the Canadian war effort is www.thegreatwar.ca, with pages devoted to the major battles in which Canadian troops were engaged. There are also many useful links to other sites. Another set of links can be found at http://cefstudygroupwebsitelist.blogspot.com, which is maintained by the Canadian Expeditionary Force Study Group. The Group itself maintains a discussion forum at http://www.cefresearch.com/phpBB2/index.php.

If you are interested in researching a Canadian soldier, then http://freepages.genealogy.rootsweb.com/~brett/cef/cefpapertrail.html#top may help, by explaining the paperwork one might come across in his personal file. The records themselves are with Library and Archives Canada and the attestation papers for each of the 600,000 men (but not the full service record) can be downloaded for free at http://www.collectionscanada.ca/archivianet/cef/index-e.html. LAC has also put war diaries for Canadian units online at http://www.collectionscanada.ca/archivianet/020152_e.html and there is a link to a slightly disappointing exhibition, supposedly about the diaries.

The most famous battle of the war in which the Canadians fought was at Vimy Ridge, where the newly restored monument can be seen for miles across the flat French countryside. http://pages.interlog.com/~fatjack/vimy/vimy.html has photographs and some letters from those who were there.

www.harrypalmergallery.ab.ca/galwareur1/galwareur1.html has photographs of the cemeteries on the Western Front that hold Canadian war dead.

No Listhttp://www.shiawasseehistory.com/cox.html has transcripts of an ordinary Gunner, George Cox, who served with the Royal Canadian Artillery between 1916 and 1919. Another Gunner was Harold S Gamblin. He recounted his memories of his time in the forces to his daughter, and transcripts of the tapes can be found at http://www.gamblinfamily.org/html/HS_Gamblin_WW1.pdf.

No Listhttp://uk.geocities.com/vimy_ridge@btinternet.com tells the story of Pte Percy Forsey, Royal Regiment of Canada, who was killed at Vimy Ridge in April 1917. From the prairies came William Peden, 8th Royal Winnipeg Rifles. His memoirs are at http://www.hcpconsulting.ca/granddad/hist002.htm.

New Zealand

A brief introduction to the New Zealand war effort is at www.nzhistory.net.nz/war/ww1-overview and an introductory look at the NZ Army during the war can be found at www.militarybadges.info/nz-army/page/07a-ww1.htm. There is also a link to the facsimile of a 1917 book, *New Zealand at the Front*.

http://freepages.genealogy.rootsweb.com/~sooty is a general NZ genealogy website with pages of rolls of honour and much else about the Kiwi effort during the First World War.

After service at Gallipoli many Kiwis experienced the horrors of the Western Front. Many seriously wounded men were sent back to Blighty to recover, especially No. 1 General Hospital at Brockenhurst, in the heart of the New Forest. www.southernlife.org.uk/nzindex.htm tells the story of the hospital. A companion site for the No. 2 Hospital at Walton upon Thames is at www.angelfire.com/ego/walton-on-thames/mf.htm.

Fiji

http://www.freewebs.com/fiji tells the story of the war effort of the Pacific

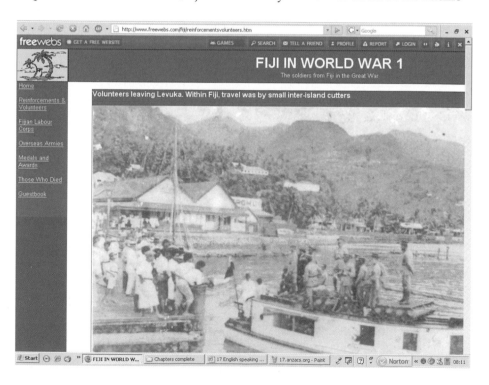

colony of Fiji, particularly that of the small European population who sent a company of men to join the British Army.

United States

One of the best introductions to the American military effort during the First World War can be found at www.newrivernotes.com//ww1, with lots of pages about the US Army and Army Air Corps, and links to other sites concerning the country's involvement in the war.

http://freepages.genealogy.rootsweb.com/~gregkrenzelok/veterinary%20c orp%20in%20ww1/veterinary%20corp%20in%20ww1.html is an interesting site about the US Veterinary Corps and the webmaster's grandfather, Sgt Leonard Patrick Murphy, and his service in the Corps. There is a very bright blue background and strange layout, which rather detracts from some fascinating material.

http://cdf-oregon.com/cdf/ww1/2nd-engrs.htm tells the history of the US 2nd Regiment of Engineers, which fought at most of the big battles of 1918.

www.lib.virginia.edu/small/exhibits/mcconnell/intro.html has transcripts of letters and papers from James Rogers McConnell, an American volunteer ambulance driver and later one of the first pilots in the Escadrille Lafayette, in France, between 1915 and 1917.

www.valloe.com/ww1/ww1.htm is a Danish site telling the story of the Frederiksen and Christoffersen families who fought with the Australians and the Americans in the First World War and the Canadians in the Second. There are pages on the Battle of Boileau Wood in July 1918.

Second World War

With the exception of Southern Ireland, the dominions declared war on Germany within a few days of the British declaration on 3 September 1939. India and the colonies joined the War at the same time as the United Kingdom. The efforts of the Commonwealth throughout the conflict were stupendous both in the men (and women) who fought alongside their British cousins in all the theatres of operations and in the munitions and raw materials supplied to help the Allied war effort.

America formally only joined the Allies on 7 December 1941 after the Japanese attack on Pearl Harbor – a day which as President Franklin Roosevelt said 'will live for ever in infamy'. In fact the US was already actively supporting Britain through the supply of equipment, protecting convoys leaving US waters and many volunteers joined the British or Canadian services. After the Japanese attack the Americans quickly became the major force among the Western Allies, through the size of their armed forces and war economy, playing the major role in defeating Japan and a leading role in beating the Germans and Italy.

Australia

A good general site about Australia during the war is http://home.st.net.au/~dunn, which looks at the war, both at home and overseas. Various pages relating to Australian, British and American forces based in Australia during the war are at www.ozatwar.com with ORBATs, brief histories, and descriptions of where they were based.

http://home.st.net.au/~dunn/tv@war.htm describes the experiences of Townsville, a sleepy town in central Queensland during the war.

A nominal roll of the million or so men and women who served in Australian forces and merchant marine during the war can be found at www.ww2roll.gov.au.

www.montevideomaru.info is about the Australian campaign in New Guinea and New Britain, and in particular the loss of over 1,000 Australian POWs in the *Montevideo Maru*, which was torpedoed by an American submarine in July 1942.

http://pow.larkin.net.au contains the experiences of Signaller Frank Larkin, a prisoner of the Japanese in the Far East, with a lot about Australian prisoners of war in the area.

http://home.vicnet.net.au/~mildura is an attractive site on the men who served aboard the corvette, HMAS *Mildura*.

www.adf-serials.com is an index to Australian military aircraft serial numbers and aircraft history, briefly describing the careers of individual aircraft. Although mainly about the Second World War, there are pages for the Royal Australian Air Force (RAAF) since 1921.

Details of military crashes in Australia during the war can be found at http://home.st.net.au/~dunn/ozcrashes.htm. There is even a list of the ten worst crashes, for those who like a lot of gore.

www.fortunecity.com/meltingpot/statuepark/620/liberator.html is about the Liberator (Mitchell B-24) aircraft flown by Australian units. A related site is at www.rnc.com.au/b-24.

A detailed history of 3 Squadron RAAF is at www.3squadron.org.au.

www.gordonstooke.com/460squadron has pages on 460 Squadron RAAF, which served in Bomber Command during the Second World War, flying the most sorties with the most casualties and winning the most decorations of any Squadron in the Command. Other sites about the squadron is at www.460squadronraaf.com, and less usefully at http://home.st.net.au/~dunn/460sqdn.htm.

www.467463raafsquadrons.com is a comprehensive site about 463 and 467 Squadrons RAAF, which were bomber squadrons in England. There are also extracts from the operation record books.

Canada

An introductory site on Canada's role in the war is at www.wwii.ca. It is good on facts and figures but otherwise rather thin on content.

www.mapleleafup.org is a slightly strange site about the equipment used by Canadian forces during the Second World War.

Camp X in Ontario trained spies and special forces for service in Europe. There is now a museum with a website at http://webhome.idirect.com/~lhodgson/camp-x.htm.

http://members.tripod.com/~merchantships/cprships1.html provides a history of Canadian Pacific ships during the war.

The rather messy homepage for the Royal Canadian Air Force Museum in Ontario is at www.rcafmuseum.on.ca. The Museum is being rebuilt, perhaps the same is happening to the website? Even so, there are some useful history pages about the equipment and the men.

www.worldchat.com/public/larkspur/index.htm tells the story of RCAF aircrew attached to the USAAF 12th Bomber Group in the Middle East during 1942 and 1943.

6 (Canadian) Group, Bomber Command, based in Yorkshire, flew hundreds of missions between 1943 and the end of the war. Find out more at www.rcaf.com/6group/left.html.

www3.sympatico.ca/angels_eight provides information on 127 Wing and associated Squadrons (mainly from the RCAF) during the Normandy Campaign.

417 (RCAF) Squadron was the only Canadian squadron in the Desert Air Force. Pages about it are at www.budslawncare.com/417.

http://dymndman.tripod.com/RCAF_424.html is the slow-to-load website devoted to 424 Squadron.

New Zealand

www.balagan.org.uk/war/nz/1939/index.htm is mainly a wargaming site, but there are some articles on the Kiwi effort during the Second World War. Much of the military heritage of Wellington was built during the war and is now disappearing. http://capitaldefence.orcon.net.nz discusses what survives and what has gone.

www.ngatoa.com/news.php has pages on the oral history of New Zealand's Second World War servicemen, with over 150 interviews on a handsome site.

http://au.geocities.com/third_div tells the almost forgotten story of 3rd NZ Division, which fought in the Solomon Islands in the Pacific. Rather text heavy, although there is a page of home snaps. There are also Excel files containing muster rolls for men who served with the Division.

www.angelfire.com/nd/domneal/powar.html is about John Thomas Murray, 7th Anti-Tank Regiment, who was taken prisoner on Crete and spent four years as a German prisoner of war.

www.cambridgeairforce.org.nz is a handsome site devoted to the city of Cambridge in central North Island, and the RNZAF units based there and nearby. There are many general pages related to the RNZAF and some useful links as well.

United States

http://memory.loc.gov/ammem/fsowhome.html contains photographs taken by the Office of War Information during the war. An on-line exhibition based on the collection is at www.loc.gov/exhibits/boundforglory/glory-exhibit.html.

The American Authentic History Center has many on-line resources at www.authentichistory.com/ww2.html, including radio broadcasts and popular music of the period.

If you are researching GIs then www.militaryindexes.com/worldwartwo has links to databases and other resources about individual service personnel.

A selection of maps, mainly for the Pacific theatre, can be found at www.lib.utexas.edu/maps/historical/history_ww2.html. The *Tampa Tribune* has put a three-dimensional version of the famous photograph of the raising of the US flag on Iwo Jima at http://multimedia.tbo.com/flash/iwojima3d/index.htm. You probably have to be crossed-eyed to get full benefit!

Red, White, Black And Blue is a recent documentary about the Japanese invasion of Alaska in 1942: the first landing of enemy forces on American soil since the British during the War of 1812! The film's website, www.alaskainvasion.com/home.html, contains interviews with veterans and other material. Unusually, the Flash introduction is worth seeing rather than skipping to the main site itself.

www.super6th.org is the comprehensive site for the 6th Armored Division, which was with General Patton in Europe.

www.100thww2.org/index.html contains some interesting pages about the 100th Infantry Division, which fought in southern France and Germany.

A unique feature of www.6thcorpscombatengineers.com is a selection of popular songs from the period, which you can even listen to as you surf. More seriously, the site provides a detailed history of the units in the 6th Corps Combat Engineers.

www.usswashington.com/dl_index.htm combines a timeline of the Second World War (at least from December 1941) with a detailed account of the activities of USS *Washington*.

The story of the US Merchant Marine, and the men who served in it, is told at www.usmm.org.

http://home.att.net/~C.C.Jordan/index.html has various essays and accounts of the USAAF in action and the airplanes it flew. Also of interest is www.worldwar2pilots.com, which contains memories of a group of veteran pilots that meet regularly in Santa Rosa, California, although it is strangely designed.

You can download wartime training films for American aircraft, and short propaganda films made about the USAAF, at www.zenoswarbirdvideos.com. It is quick to do, but unfortunately the quality is poor.

www.pointvista.com/WW2GliderPilots/index.htm has many pages about American Glider Pilots, including a roll of honour for those killed in action.

The story of the Martin B-26 Marauder fighter-bomber and pages about the men who served in them is at www.b26.com/index.html.

www.littlefriends.co.uk is dedicated to the 8th Army Air Force Fighter Command, which flew from bases in England. There is a museum at Savannah, Georgia, with a website at www.mightyeighth.org.

www.enter.net/~rocketeer/13thmain.html has many pages on the 13th Air Force, which served in the Pacific Theatre, as well as the restoration of a vintage, Second World War jeep.

The history of 94th Bomb Group is told at www.94thbombgroup.com. The Group mainly flew missions from Rougham, near Bury St Edmunds, but the site is largely about veterans' reunions.

www.parhamairfieldmuseum.co.uk/390home.html has pages devoted to 390th Bomb Group, 8th USAAF, who flew from Parham in Suffolk.

http://rougham.org is dedicated to preserving the control tower at former RAF Rougham in Suffolk, which was home to the USAAF 322nd and 94th Bomb Groups.

www.ixengineercommand.com is a very detailed site about IX Engineer Command, which built airfields for the USAAF in Britain and Europe.

The Skylighters website www.skylighters.org is a superbly laid out and well resourced site about the 225th Anti-Aircraft Searchlight Battalion between D-Day and VE Day.

Chapter 17

EUROPEAN AND OTHER ALLIES

First World War

The contribution of Britain's allies to the ultimate victory in 1918 has often been overshadowed, but the Battle of Verdun, which took place over the spring and summer of 1916, was perhaps the bloodiest battle fought during

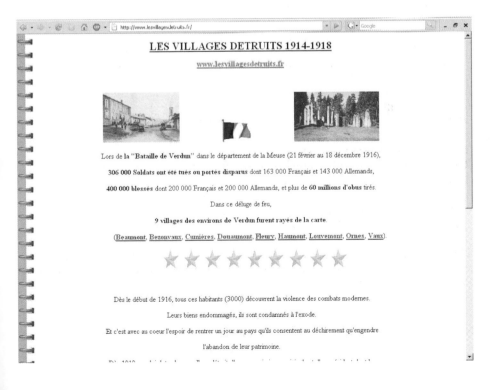

http://www.lesvillagesdetruits.fr/

LES VILLAGES DETRUITS 1914-1918

www.lesvillagesdetruits.fr

Lors de la "Bataille de Verdun" dans le département de la Meuse (21 février au 18 décembre 1916),

306 000 Soldats ont été tués ou portés disparus dont 163 000 Français et 143 000 Allemands,

400 000 blessés dont 200 000 Français et 200 000 Allemands, et plus de **60 millions d'obus** tirés.

Dans ce déluge de feu,

9 villages des environs de Verdun furent rayés de la carte.

(Beaumont, Bezonvaux, Cumières, Douaumont, Fleury, Haumont, Louvemont, Ornes, Vaux).

★ ★ ★ ★ ★ ★ ★ ★ ★

Dès le début de 1916, tous ces habitants (3000) découvrent la violence des combats modernes.

Leurs biens endommagés, ils sont condamnés à l'exode.

Et c'est avec au coeur l'espoir de rentrer un jour au pays qu'ils consentent au déchirement qu'engendre

l'abandon de leur patrimoine.

the war, with far more casualties than the Somme, which was originally planned as a diversion. Although it was a victory, the campaign bled the French Army dry, and led to mutinies by the *Poilus* (ordinary soldiers).

Fort Liezele is a museum in a restored Belgian fort on the outskirts of Antwerp, which was occupied by the Germans in September 1914, the website is at http://users.pandora.be/bart.van.bulck/start.html.

http://ccsc.genealogie.free.fr/Plaques/Plaques.htm is a French site (in French but it is easy to work out what is going on) with lots of contemporary photographs about the French troops, mainly at the Yser (in Belgium). http://batmarn2.club.fr/menuseng.htm is a French site, in English, devoted to the 1918 Battle of the Marne.

The greatest battle engaged in by French forces was the defence of Verdun. www.lesvillagesdetruits.fr.st (in French) has pages, with many photographs, about the villages that were destroyed during the fighting. http://web.telia.com/~u58602288/index.htm is a Swedish site devoted to Verdun, with lots of photographs of how the battlefield looks today.

One of the creepiest war memorials ever built is the Ossuary at Douaumont, which contains the bones of tens of thousands of French and German war dead. More about it can be found at www.verdun-douaumont.com/en/index.html.
The Italian experience of the war is told at www.grandeguerra.com. Unfortunately, the site is entirely in Italian.

Second World War

In 1945 the United Nations was formed with 50 members, overwhelmingly countries who joined the British, Americans and Russians in their defeat of the Axis powers. Some, of course, were Dominions (and websites about their war effort can be found in Chapter 16), while others, mainly in South America, contributed little or nothing to the Allied victory.

If you are interested in how the Second World War affected the smaller nations, then http://members.tripod.com/~marcin_w/index-2.html might help, for it has pages on most countries and their armed forces, which participated in the war in one way or another. To get to the other pages you need to scroll to the very bottom of this page. Sadly, it is rather out of date and needs updating.

Apart from the British Isles, Portugal, Spain, Sweden and Switzerland all European countries were either members of the Axis (see Chapter 18) or occupied by their troops. There are a number of websites about their experiences.

Belgium

Belgium was occupied in May 1940 and most parts of the country were liberated in the autumn of 1944. There seems to be nothing online, in English at least, about the country's experiences, which revealed a deeply divided country. Instead, webmasters have concentrated on the positive aspects. Perhaps the best place to start is at http://noviomagus.tripod.com, which looks at a remarkable Belgian lady, Marthe E Janssen-Leyder, who helped British and Allied escapers and evaders from her home near the Dutch border.

Although mainly in Dutch, www.forten.info/index.htm is a site devoted to fortifications in the Low Countries. Although it is not indicated, a number of pages are in English, particularly those about the Atlantic Wall. There are also a number of links to other sites devoted to the history of fortifications worldwide.

Another similar site is www.fortweb.net/photos, which is devoted to photographs of fortresses across Europe, including the Atlantic Wall and forts in Liège and Antwerp.

A brief history of the Belgian Air Force during the war is at http://members.tripod.com/~John_C_McLeod/BL.htm. There are also a few pages about Belgians in 219 Squadron, RAF.

Some 700 Belgian aircrew served in the RAF or the SAAF, escaping from Belgium or undertaking a hazardous journey from the Congo. Their story is told at www.bamfbamrs.be/RAF/index.htm, and there is a list of names.

In the RAF, 96 pilots served with 350 (Belgian) Fighter Squadron RAF. More about the Squadron and its exploits can be found at http://users.skynet.be/bonge.gemoets/index.htm.

http://users.skynet.be/jo.boone/index.htm contains a number of very interesting photographs about Belgium and its occupation by the Germans (with some material for the First World War as well) taken by amateur photographers.

Brazil

Brazil was the only South American country that actively participated in the war. Troops and aircraft were despatched in 1943 and 1944 to fight in Italy. Their story is told at www.closecombat.org/BrClan/HC/brazil_goes_to_war.htm. More about the Brazilian air effort, particularly the 1st Brazilian Air Group, which flew as part of the US 12th Air Force, can be found at www.rudnei.cunha.nom.br/FAB/en.

Czechoslovakia

Czechoslovakia was the first victim of the Second World War, being dismembered and then occupied by the Germans in the autumn of 1938 and spring 1939. It was finally liberated in May 1945. A number of Czechs escaped to the west, and http://cz-raf.hyperlink.cz is about Czech airmen in the RAF (the text is in both English and Czech). Another website on the same subject is www.rogerdarlington.me.uk/czechsinraf.htm, which largely consists of extracts from the book *Night Hawks*, written by the website owner in the mid-1980s. However, there are links to an *Observer* newspaper article about the Czech Nazi agent, Augustin Preucil, who flew with the RAF in 1940 and 1941.

Denmark

Although Danish webmasters have posted a number of attractive websites about the Second World War, they seem curiously reluctant to put up one relating to their own country's experience. The only site I have found (in English at least) is www.danishww2pilots.dk, which is about the Danish pilots who fought during the Second World War on both sides, although most, naturally, chose the Allies.

France

France is another country that seems reluctant to discuss its wartime history online, again perhaps because it is still a very sensitive subject.

http://perso.orange.fr/lepoilu/ww2/ww2history.htm offers a short, one-page account of the French forces that fought on the side of the Allies. More informative is http://france1940.free.fr, a site in English and French devoted to the Fall of France in 1940, and French forces during the Second World War as a whole. Unfortunately, as the webmaster wryly admits, great chunks of it is still 'under construction'. Even so, it is a useful introduction.

Famously, the Maginot Line along the French–German border was meant to prevent a German attack, but remains a symbol of backwards military thinking, as it was easily circumnavigated during the Blitzkrieg of May 1940. www.maginot67.com/intro.htm is a weirdly laid out site about the Maginot line, mainly in French. There is also a selection of photos, taken by the webmaster's father, of an American raid on Strasbourg in August 1944.

In 1941 Charles de Gaulle established the Order of Liberation. The French Museum of the Order of Liberation's website at www.ordredelaliberation.fr/english/contenido1.php commemorates the 1,036 men and women who were awarded the honour, plus a little about the less prestigious Order of the Resistance.

Netherlands

Alone of the occupied countries, the Dutch have a large number of websites devoted to the Dutch experience during the Second World War, many of which have English pages. This may be because the war here was a unifying experience, with little collaboration, unlike in other nations.

Perversely, let's start with a handsome site that is entirely in Dutch, www.leger1939–1940.nl, which looks at the Netherlands during the Phoney War of 1939–1940. Even if your Dutch is negligible, there are lots of photos, postcards and other illustrations to enable you to get a feel for what service in the armed forces was like. However, if you can't face this, www.geocities.com/M_van_bockel is about the equipment, particularly those used by the motorised units, in the Dutch Army in 1940. And it is in English. You might also find www.geocities.com/Pentagon/Barracks/1247, an ORBAT of the Dutch Army at the time of the German invasion, worth a visit.

The Germans seem to have had little trouble with the M38 Armoured Car. Of the 12 available in May 1940, eight saw action, two of them unarmed. The other four were probably at Eindhoven awaiting modification and repairs – www.landsverk-m38.nl reports on a project to restore one of the surviving cars.

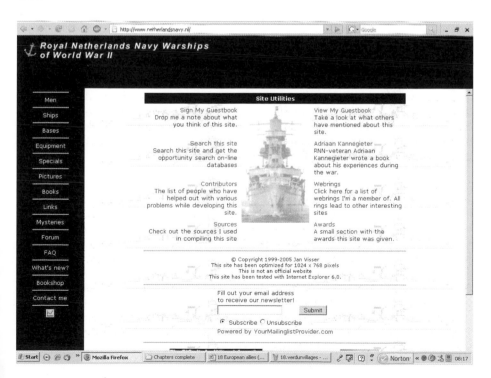

After the occupation the Dutch quickly got used to seeing fleets of Allied bombers passing overhead on their way to bomb targets in Germany. Inevitably, some planes crashed over the Netherlands, brought down by enemy action or mechanical failure. www.crash40–45.nl/index_uk.html is a Dutch site investigating crashes of aircraft around Amsterdam. More generally, www.airwarweb.net is a comprehensive site devoted to the air war over the Netherlands, with pages about Dutch pilots in the RAF and the *Luftwaffe*, and the recovery of crashed aircraft.

A number of Dutch naval vessels escaped to England after the invasion. Their story is told at www.netherlandsnavy.nl, which also includes the history of individual ships and something about the men on them as well.

The Netherlands East Indies (Indonesia) was invaded by the Japanese at the end of 1941. The Dutch, and the British and Australian troops who arrived to help defend the islands, put up a valiant but futile resistance. www.geocities.com/dutcheastindies is a detailed and well written account of the campaign in the Dutch East Indies during 1941 and 1942. Many atrocities were committed by the Japanese, chief of which was the construction of the Pakan-Baroe 'death railway' across Sumatra, built by Indonesian natives, Dutch civilians and other Allied POWs. Its story is movingly told at http://au.geocities.com/frans_taminiau. A number of airmen escaped and found their way to Australia, where they were joined by the Netherlands East Indies Air Force (NEI-AF), under Australian control. More about this can be found at http://home.st.net.au/~dunn/nei-af.htm.

Norway

The Nazis invaded Norway in April 1940, followed by a hurried and ill-conceived British and French counter-invasion around Narvik, in the north of the country. The resulting shambles was the major reason why Neville Chamberlain was forced to resign, although part of the blame must be laid at the feet of Winston Churchill as First Lord of the Admiralty. An increasingly unpopular German occupation was only lifted in May 1945.

The Norwegian resistance movement was supported by the famous 'Shetland Bus', which ferried men and supplies from the Shetland Islands to the fjords of Norway, and which is commemorated at www.shetland-heritage.co.uk/shetlandbus. There is also a page about life in Norway itself in wartime.

As elsewhere, webmasters have tended to focus on aerial activities. http://folk.uio.no/hungnes/avia/noavia/norw.htm looks at Norwegian airmen and Norwegian Squadrons in the RAF. http://home.no.net/thsord has details of several hundred air crashes (both Allied and German) in southern Norway. Meanwhile, www.stormbirds.com/eagles looks at the experience of the *Luftwaffe* in Norway.

Poland

With the possible exception of Russia, no country suffered more during the Second World War than Poland. It was invaded on 1 September 1939 and then within a few weeks brutally and cynically divided between Nazi Germany and the Soviet Union. Millions of Poles were killed or made homeless and at the end of the war, the country was literally moved 150km to the west.

It is arguable that the late intervention of fresh Polish (and Czech) squadrons proved to be the turning point during the Battle of Britain. And to add humiliation to tragedy, they were the only nation not permitted to march in London's Victory Parade in July 1946, for fear of upsetting the Russians.

Despite the fact that many links are broken, www.ostrycharz.free-online.co.uk/PolishLinks.html is perhaps the best place to start, as it has much about the Polish experience during the War. As the URL suggests, www.polishsoldier.co.uk provides a detailed examination of the Polish formations that fought in the West, and in particular, their heroism.

An interesting and informative website devoted to the Polish Resistance (Home Army) is at http://polishresistance-ak.org. It was the largest resistance movement in Europe and was behind the ill-fated Warsaw Uprising in the summer of 1944. The tragedy of the Uprising is well described at www.warsawuprising.com.

Other sites tend to concentrate on Poles in the air. At its peak strength, the Polish Air Force was the largest Allied air force based in the UK after the RAF and USAAF, with 15 Squadrons and many training and support units. www.geocities.com/skrzydla/index.html is, for example, a comprehensive site about Polish squadrons in the RAF. www.btinternet.com/~aquila/lincs/polishaf/paf.htm offers detailed information about Polish squadrons in Lincolnshire.

There were 40 or so Polish air aces, that is, pilots who managed to shoot down five or more enemy aircraft. Their exploits are described at http://members.tripod.com/~marcin_w/index-paces.html, all of whom, the site is at pains to stress, were ethnic Poles. Perhaps more interesting is www.wojciechowski.freeserve.co.uk/miw/index.htm, which is the biography of a Polish pilot, Miroslav Wojciechowski (1917–1956), who served in 303 (Polish) Squadron RAF and remained in the post-war RAF.

Soviet Union (Russia)

It is only since the collapse of the Soviet Union and the end of the Cold War in the early 1990s that the true and epic nature of the battles and campaigns on the Eastern Front have been revealed, as the archives have opened and veterans have felt free to talk about their experiences. Russia was invaded on 21 June 1941 (after an alliance with the Nazis). This came as a complete surprise to Stalin, although he had been repeatedly warned that an attack was imminent. Indeed, I have seen a copy of a minute from a Soviet spy, across which Stalin scrawled a very rude Russian word! Aided by the weather and increasingly bizarre tactics imposed by Hitler on the Nazi forces, the Russians managed to regroup, rearm, and eventually push the Germans west, reaching Berlin in early May 1945. It was not a pretty or chivalrous war, as a number of these websites show.

Pobediteli (Russian for 'victors') is an extremely impressive multimedia site devoted to the Great Patriotic War at http://english.pobediteli.ru. There are interviews with veterans, timelines and a database to the million or so veterans still alive. Even with broadband it is slow to load, but you should visit this site.

Less conventional is www.wio.ru (the URL stands for War is Over), which describes the Soviet armed forces during the Second World War. There are also other pages devoted to the Russian and Soviet forces during the First World War and the inter-war period. A similar site is www.battlefield.ru, although there is more of an emphasis on armoured vehicles.

Indeed, the Soviet victory was due, in large part, to the superior armoured vehicles, particularly the feared T34 tank. If you want to know more, then a good place to start is the website of the Russian Military Historical Museum of Armoured Vehicles and Equipment at Kubinka. Its website at www.tankmuseum.ru has lots of pages devoted to Russian and Soviet tanks and military vehicles with some stunning and unique photographs.

There are fewer sites about the air war. One French site (in French) at www.pascalguillerm.fr is about the air war on the Eastern Front, with profiles of both *Luftwaffe* and Red Air Force aces. A fascinating site about the female air aces of the Soviet Air Forces is at http://pratt.edu/~rsilva/sovwomen.htm, with another website about the 58,000 women who served with the Soviet forces at http://lonestar.texas.net/~snolep/topicalpg/index05.htm. Another site with pages on the air war is at www.bergstrombooks.elknet.pl/bc-rs. It is mainly pushing a rather expensive series of books, probably of most interest to the specialist.

Lastly, a very eccentric and rather moving site about one ordinary Russian man's experiences during the war can be found at http://ldb1.narod.ru/index2.html. Unfortunately, it is rather slow loading, with some pages in fractured English.

The most famous battle was the epic struggle at Stalingrad over the winter of 1942/43. Some photographs, taken by Swedish military enthusiasts on a recent visit to the battlefield, are at http://web.telia.com/~u58602288/index.htm.

Yugoslavia

Yugoslavia was invaded in April 1941. The campaign, and the subsequent occupation of Greece, took roughly two months, which delayed the launch Operation Barbarossa by the same time period, meaning that the Germans had two months less to defeat the Soviet Union. This delay proved fatal to Nazi ambitions. During the war itself the resistance movement was badly split between the Chetniks, loyal to the Royal Family, and the Communists under Marshal Tito, who, to the frustration of the Western Allies, seemed to spend as much time fighting each other as the Germans. A comprehensive site about the War in Yugoslavia is at www.vojska.net/eng/world-war-2. A brief history of the Yugoslav Partisan Air Force, the one organised by a partisan organisation during the war, is at http://members.tripod.com/~marcin_w/index-jpaf.html.

Chapter 18

ENEMY POWERS

Until recently the First World War (and to a lesser extent, the Second World War) has largely been seen from an almost exclusively Anglophone perspective. Both the effectiveness and motivation of the German enemy and our French ally were hardly considered by historians. Fortunately, this attitude is slowly changing – in part because other countries are becoming just as fascinated by the world wars as the British are themselves – and this is reflected in cyberspace with an increasing number of websites.

First World War

www.viribusunitis.ca is a detailed site about the Austro-Hungarian battleship *Viribus Unitis* and her sister ships, with photos, drawings and a history.

www.turkeyswar.com is a site that looks at the Turkish Army during the First World War, with a lot of information about the battles, the soldiers and the equipment. At the time of writing it was closed for maintenance.

Originally for collectors of German military helmets, www.pickelhauben.net/articles/Landsturm.html, has spread to include many pages about the German Army before and during the First World War. It is probably more use for English speakers than www.forum14–18.de, another site devoted to the German Army in the First World War, which is all in German.

www.kaiserlicherautomobilclub.de/english/inhalt.html is an unusual site devoted to the German Imperial Automobile Club, which had a military corps attached to it. You can listen to the Club song, 'Hurrah, Hurrah The Kaiser Is Coming', but most visitors might be more interested in the weaponry (especially the daggers) handled by club members and the uniforms they wore.

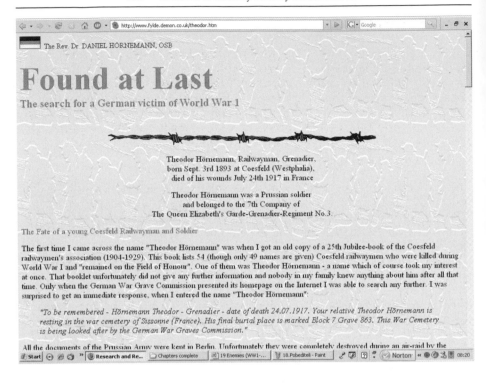

There are few pages about individual German soldiers. One exception is www.fylde.demon.co.uk/theodor.htm, which contains the research for a young German railwayman and Grenadier, Theodor Hörnemann, who was killed in July 1917, who may have been a relation of the webmaster.

http://uboat.net/wwi has many excellent pages relating to the U-boat campaign. A related site, although not as detailed, can be found at http://members.fortunecity.se/mikaelxii/ww1/Germany/fleet/submarine.html.

www.100megsfree2.com/jjscherr/scherr/vonscheer.htm contains the biography of German Admiral Reinhard von Scheer, who set up the Imperial German Navy before the First World War and then led the Home Fleet during the war itself. It is part of a wider site devoted to a history of the Scheer family. Unless you have the speakers on your computer turned off, you will be deafened by a very tinny version of the German national anthem.

www.anzacs.net/MvR_English.htm tells the detailed story of German's most famous air ace, Manfred von Richthoven, the 'Red Baron'. www.mikerlewis.com has some interesting pages about the restoration of two German aircraft – a Halberstadt CV and LVG CVI – at Brussels Air Museum.

Second World War

One of the surprising things in researching this book was discovering the large numbers of sites devoted to researching the Axis forces: that is Germany, Italy, Japan and their smaller European allies. By and large these are serious studies of the equipment and the men who fought against the British, the Americans and their Allies. There is an emphasis on air forces and the aircraft they flew, perhaps reflecting that, in many cases, they were technologically advanced, relatively unsullied by the barbarity of other Axis forces, and above all they were exciting.

There are also a number of German sites – a few of which are included – that reflect the fact that the war is now history for the vast majority of Germans. After all, almost nobody under the age of 70 would have any direct memory of the war, although, of course, because of the Holocaust and the other atrocities committed by German forces, let alone the flight of millions of German refugees from the East, the War still has (and will continue to have) a special resonance in Germany.

Even so, most webmasters stress their anti-Nazi credentials; perhaps because many visitors seemingly mistake a legitimate interest in an aspect of the Second World War with fascist sympathies. If you are interested in this you should read the page at www.geocities.com/Vienna/Strasse/8514/ history.html, explaining what the site's webmaster hopes to achieve and why he is not a Nazi. It is something that people who run other such websites probably sympathise with. The site itself offers an introduction to the Third Reich for secondary schools, with links to more detailed sites (although, irritatingly, many are broken).

A simple and impressive site to begin with is www.axishistory.com, which has pages about the German, Japanese and Italian war efforts, as well as those of the smaller Axis powers, from Bulgaria to Slovakia. It also looks at collaborator organisations in occupied countries.

The Axis air forces are discussed in the Sturmvogel website at www.geocities.com/CapeCanaveral/2072/index.html. Perhaps the most useful pages are for Axis orders of battle (ORBATs) for various periods of the war.

Germany

If you are looking for a general introduction to the armed forces of Germany, then www.feldgrau.com is an excellent place to begin. An unusual feature is that it also contains material about the truncated Army and Navy (the Air Force was banned) maintained by the country during the Weimar Republic between 1919 and 1933.

Wehrmacht

Although largely in German www.diedeutschewehrmacht.de is an introduction to the Wehrmacht, with plenty of ORBATs, which are much the same in any language.

The pride of the *Wehrmacht* were the Panzer units, which spearheaded the Blitzkrieg into Poland, France and Russia. A Danish site – www.panzerworld.net – provides all you need to know about German Panzers and a lot more besides, including the costs of individual tanks and guns, as well as salaries and benefits for German soldiers and their families. Another comprehensive site on the same topic is www.achtungpanzer.com. Meanwhile, http://home.hetnet.nl/~conny-rene/1epaginaframeset.html is devoted to the 7th Panzer Division, which fought mainly on the Eastern Front.

The memoirs of a Lt Wilhelm Radovsky, a German officer, in Russia can be found at www.wilhelm-radkovsky.de. The site is in German.

The most feared troops however were the SS. The story of the 2nd Division ('Das Reich'), *Waffen*-SS, is told at www.dasreich.ca.

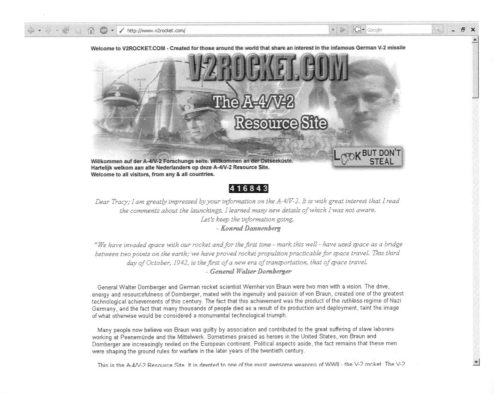

www.frundsberg10.com is the website of an American living history association, which recreates the 10th Division, Waffen-SS unit. Strangely designed, it is best to use the frames to make sense of it. There are links to other Allied and Axis re-enactment units in North America and Europe.

As the URL suggests, www.v2rocket.com looks at the V2s (sometimes referred as the A4) that were fired at England during late 1944 and almost until the German surrender in May 1945. There is even a video you can download of a test firing. And in addition, there is also a little bit about the American tests after the war.

Kriegsmarine
Two similar Danish sites offer details about three of the battleships built and maintained by the German Navy: www.kbismarck.com is an informative site about the German battleship *Bismarck* and the men who served aboard her. Meanwhile, www.scharnhorst-class.dk is a comprehensive site about the German battleships *Gneisenau* and *Scharnhorst*. Less informative are the related sites www.admiral-hipper-class.dk and www.deutschland-class.dk.

www.u-35.com is devoted to the story of the men from U-35, which was sunk in November 1939. Its crew then spent the rest of the war as prisoners in England and Canada.

Luftwaffe
If you are researching the *Luftwaffe*, then the first port of call has to be www.lwag.org/index.php, the home of the *Luftwaffe* Archives and Reference Group – a collective of researchers who share their information online. The Group was founded in June 2000 by a loose-knit crowd of 50 prominent aviation archivists, historians, webmasters and authors, all specialising in the German Air Force during the Second World War. You will need to scroll down the home page to find links to the webpages maintained by members, including discussion pages.

www.stormbirds.com is another confederation of related websites. Some of these sites are somewhat specialised, however.

An attractive and easy to use introduction to the *Luftwaffe* is at www.ww2.dk, with brief histories of units, both flying and ground, and descriptions of some of the aircraft flown. There are several websites devoted to the history of individual *Jagdgeschwader*, which were units roughly equivalent to squadrons in RAF Fighter Command. www.lesbutler.ip3.co.uk/jg26/schlageter.htm is about Jagdgeschwader 26, which flew in Western Europe, and includes maps and lists of casualties. Another site on the unit is at http://members.cox.net/schlageter1.

www.jagdgeschwader52.de/seitegb.htm is a German site about Jagdgeschwader 52, which fought on the Eastern Front, although there are many pages in English, while www.jg54greenhearts.com offers a comprehensive site on another unit that also saw service in Russia, Jagdgeschwader 54.

The greatest *Luftwaffe* air ace of the war was Adolph Galland (1912–1996). http://members.aol.com/geobat66/galland/galland.htm provides a sympathetic and comprehensive biography. There are several sites about the other German aces. In particular, http://hem2.passagen.se/galland has material about a number of Luftwaffe air aces. Other sites covering much the same topic are www.luftwaffe.cz/index.html and www.pilotenbunker.de (which has a number of pages in English). www.pascalguillerm.fr is a French site (in French) about the air war on the Eastern Front, with profiles of both Luftwaffe and Red Air Force aces, but it is fairly easy to glean information.

Prisoners Of War

www.kriegsgefangen.de started in February 2001 with the intention of documenting German POWs in American hands. However, because most Germans were not held by the Americans, the webmaster has adding an increasing amount of information on, in his words, 'the scarcely documented history of German prisoners of war all over the world'. The site is in German and slightly fractured English.

There are several British websites that study German POW camps: www.powcamp.com is the website for Harperley Museum in Co. Durham, which is based around a former German POW Camp. Rather more interesting is www.islandfarm.fsnet.co.uk/index.html, an extremely comprehensive site about the Island Farm POW Camp near Bridgend, which saw the largest escape of German POWs during the Second World War in March 1945, with useful pages about tracing the history of other German POW camps and a map showing their location.

Home Front

There are a couple of sites about quasi-military organisations. As the URL suggests, www.germanpolice.org is an informative site about the German police during the Third Reich, with information about structure, uniforms and miscellaneous items such as postcards. However, it is somewhat strangely arranged.

Another informative resource relates to the Bund Deutsche Maedel – the female equivalent to the *Hitlerjügend* – at www.bdmhistory.com, with digitised examples of training manuals, magazines and many photographs. There are even pages dedicated to a re-enactment group.

A strange site is at www.wastedyears.eu/category/news, about the making of the Belgian documentary and animated feature *Wasted Years*, about a teenager's experiences of Nazi Germany. It is still very much work in progress.

There are a number of sites, largely in German, relating to the war in Germany itself. Probably the best place to start is the Deutsche Welle (the equivalent of the BBC World Service) microsite in English, at www6.dw-world.de/en/worldwarII.php. Other sites include www.historisches-centrum.de/index.php?id=325, which is devoted to the Battle of the Ruhr in 1945 (with a few pages in English) and http://luftfahrtspuren.de, a very informative site about the war in the air over Schleswig-Holstein.

A facsimile of the surrender document signed at Reims on 7 May 1945 can be found at www.footnote.com/viewer.php?image=4346739.

Axis Forces

Although the Germans were the dominant party, the Axis consisted of a number of other countries.

Finland was never formally a member, but was a co-belligerent. It fought two separate wars against the Soviet Union in 1939–1940 (the Winter War) and 1941–1944 (the Continuation War). A detailed history of the Finnish Air Force, which played a key role, can be found at www.sci.fi/~ambush/faf/faf.html. There are also pages devoted to the post-war history of the Air Force.

The Italians were much derided at the time and subsequently. However, http://comandosupremo.com considers the Italian military contribution to the Second World War in depth and argues that this derision is largely a result of British propaganda. Meanwhile, www.geocities.com/Pentagon/Quarters/1975/carristi.htm discusses the range of tanks and armoured vehicles used by the Italian Army – the 'Iron Soap Boxes' as they were cruelly described by their users.

Nobody, however, mocked the Japanese fighting forces. There are several sites about them. http://maisov.oops.jp/e looks at the organisation of the Imperial Japanese Army and Navy. To access the main website you need to click on 'large indices'. Readers just interested in the Imperial Japanese Army should visit the comprehensive www3.plala.or.jp/takihome, which has many pages on organisation, weapons and insignia. A detailed site for the Imperial Japanese Navy is at www.combinedfleet.com/kaigun.htm.

An introduction to the Japanese Army and Navy air services and the aircraft they flew can be found at www.enter.net/~rocketeer/13thaaf/13thijaf.html. A more detailed site about the aircraft is at www.j-aircraft.com.

Lastly, you should not miss the very weird Strange Mechanism Museum at www.strange-mecha.com/index-e.htm, which looks at experimental weapons built by the Japanese and Germans during the 1930s and 1940s.

There are several sites about the atomic attacks on Hiroshima and Nagasaki, including www.nvccom.co.jp/abomb/fronte.html. The raids directly led to the Japanese surrender and the succinct surrender document signed by the Imperial Government on 2 September 1945 can be seen at www.footnote.com/viewer.php?image=4346690.

War Crimes

An estimated 6 million Jews and many gypsies, homosexuals and disabled people were murdered during the Holocaust, sometimes referred to as the *Shoah* (Hebrew for 'catastrophe' or 'destruction').

The Yad Vashem memorial in Jerusalem is the major repository of information about the Holocaust. It has a library of 100,000 volumes and an extensive archive containing primary source material, including many testimonies from survivors. It also maintains an on-line Central Database of Holocaust Victims at www.yadvashem.org, with details of over 3 million

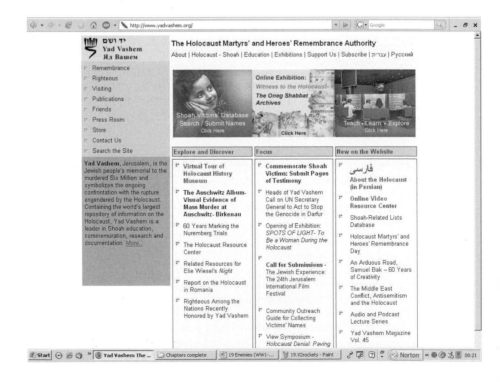

victims. The database will tell you where people came from and the camps at which they died. Using it is a sobering experience.

If you are looking for a general introduction to the subject, then www.holocaust-history.org is a good place to start. It is a free archive of documents, photographs, recordings, and essays regarding the Holocaust, including direct refutation of Holocaust-denial. Other useful introductory sites are www.death-camps.org/websites/jmain.htm and http://holocaust.klup.info, although it largely consists of links to other websites.

There are a number of more specialist sites. The Web Genocide Document Centre at www.ess.uwe.ac.uk/search.htm has lots of original documents and other material. Unfortunately, not every page opens, so you may not be able to use all the resources. The Shoah Foundation in California has videotaped interviews with survivors as well as material for teachers and students at www.usc.edu/schools/college/vhi.

An impressive site about Auschwitz and the people who died there is at www.auschwitz.dk. We tend to think that the killings went on at the big camps such as Auschwitz, Bergen-Belsen and Treblinka, but in fact millions were murdered in smaller camps that have almost been forgotten: www.jewishgen.org/forgottencamps/index.html looks at some of these places.

http://members.iinet.net.au/%7Egduncan/massacres.html tells the story of some of the massacres and atrocities that took place in Belgium, the Netherlands, France and Greece. Many of these war crimes, particularly the indiscriminate shooting of Jewish men and women, were carried out by members of the *Einsatztruppen*. There is a site devoted to them at www.einsatzgruppenarchives.com/einsatz.html, which makes horrific reading.

The Nuremburg and other war crimes trials in 1946 and subsequent years saw the conviction of many of the surviving Nazi leaders. Papers and transcripts of these trials can be found at http://nuremberg.law.harvard.edu/php/docs_swi.php?DI=1&text=overview.

Appendix I

TOP TEN MILITARY SITES

Below I have listed a selection of websites, which, in my opinion, every student of military history should bookmark. To merit inclusion they had to display scholarship and be genuinely useful to researchers. I decided not to include any sites about individual types of equipment or, with the exception of Wikipedia, general historical sites. They are in no particular order but I hope illustrate something about each one of the services and a variety of historical periods.

1. Wikipedia

The internet has produced a large number of sites where scholars and enthusiasts from around the world work together to produce something of greater value than any one individual could by themselves.

The best example of this collaboration, are wikis (apparently from a Hawaiian word *wiki wiki* meaning fast), which are websites that allows visitors to add, edit and change content. The most important of these is Wikipedia, which has some 1.7m entries in English (and hundreds of thousands of more in other languages as well). Wikipedia is often criticised for its inaccuracy and bias, but in my experience the military history articles are spot on. And in case if you spot a mistake you can always make a correction.

http://en.wikipedia.org

2. Commonwealth War Graves Commission

Since 1917 the Commonwealth War Graves Commission has been caring for war graves of men from Britain and the Commonwealth who died during the two world wars. They maintain 23,000 cemeteries across the world. Visiting

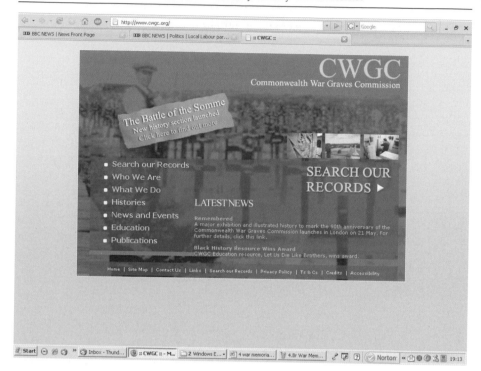

any of them is a profoundly moving experience, as their calm and immaculately kept grounds bring home the horrors and futility of war.

Their website is based on the Debt of Honour Register, which records details of the 1,750,000 men (and a few women) for whose graves they care, with 67,000 civilians who lost their lives as the result of enemy action during the Second World War. For each individual there are details of his unit, when he died and where he is buried. Often there may well be details of next of kin plus the inscription that is on the gravestone. The register will tell in which cemetery he is buried (with plot number) and how to get there. There is even a brief history of the cemetery itself. There are also pages about the history of the Commission and material for teachers.

www.cwgc.org

3. Land Forces Of Britain, The Empire And The Commonwealth

This is one of the oldest sites on the internet, having been launched as long ago as 1995. The aim was simple: to provide brief details on every Army unit that served the British Crown.

This was an ambitious project and inevitably some units are pretty well covered, while there is very little for others. One of the great strengths of this site is that it is simply laid out and easy to navigate. Each page should contain information, such as title changes and lineage, battalion service histories, battle honours, badges, lists of colonels, alliances, bibliographies, etc., as well as links to 'every' known regimental page on the internet (official, historical, biographical, re-enactment, etc.). Several features are cross-referenced to other sections of the site. For example, the battle honours for each regiment are linked to war pages, which give more information about the context of the battles and their wars. The site is designed to help you trace the changes in designations of regiments, and the complexities of their lineages.

As of 2004 there are well over 2,000 such pages. Unfortunately, the site is still incomplete and does not seem to have been updated since mid-2005. Even so, it is the first port of call if you want to find out basic facts about a British (or Canadian or Australian, etc.) Army unit.

www.regiments.org

4. The Australian War Memorial

Despite the name, the AWM, in the heart of Canberra, is one of the world's great museums. Even non-military enthusiasts can easily spend a day there and not see everything (the website has a virtual tour so you can what you are missing). Like London's Imperial War Museum it was founded to commemorate the sacrifice made by thousands of young Australian men and women during the First World War. As a result, the emphasis is very much on the people rather than the kit they used or even the battles they took part in.

In recent years the Memorial has placed a large number of databases online, ranging from a Roll of Honour to Australia's 100,000 men who died in wars since 1900; nominal rolls for men who served overseas (some actually provided by the Department of Veterans' Affairs); details of awards and honours and some information about prisoners of war. Indeed, if you are researching individuals who served in the Australian armed forces (the vast majority of whom had close family links to Britain) until the late 1960s, you should find them here. The only major exception is service records, which are now available online (at least for the First World War) from the National Archives at www.naa.gov.au.

There are also war diaries for Australian units, examples of artefacts from the collections, and a number of special exhibitions. I found the one on colour photography between 1914 and 1918 particularly interesting. There are even several blogs, but at the time of writing they were not operational.

www.awm.gov.au

5. The Asplin Military History Resources

Fortunately, the internet has room for both the highly professional websites posted by archives and museums, and those that are quite clearly labours of love by one individual or small group, and which can put the sites of much larger bodies to shame. Chief among the latter is this website, devoted to the later Victorian and Edwardian Army.

Kevin Asplin is an Army officer and medal researcher by profession. It is clear that he is not a web designer, for his site consists of three pages you scroll down to find the resource you want. The scanning of images has also led to some odd results. And perhaps most seriously, there is no index and things are rather mixed up. Does all this matter? Not really. All you need is patience and enthusiasm.

His main interest, at least initially, seems to be the Imperial Yeomanry – mounted troops who were recruited during the Boer War. There is a list of all 38,000 men who served in with the Yeomanry. Mr Asplin has been adding other resources, such as lists of men who joined colonial units during the Boer War; medal rolls for various colonial conflicts, casualty rolls for the Crimean and other wars of the period; some records for individual regiments (you will need to check to see whether yours is here), as well as a few individual soldiers; and a page describing the major sources for military research at Kew.

http://hometown.aol.co.uk/kevinasplin/home.html

6. The National Archives

You will need to visit The National Archives at Kew if you are researching almost any aspect of British military history, from a soldier's career to the development of post-war missile systems. The breadth and range of their holdings is reflected on the website, which can, at times, be difficult to navigate.

Highlights include a range of research guides explaining what records they have and how you can use them: inevitably most are aimed at family historians, but there are a few more specialist titles. They link to the on-line catalogue, which has descriptions of over 9 million documents, maps, files and parchment rolls. In some cases the catalogue contains more detailed information – for example there is a list of all soldiers for whom there are surviving pension documents between 1760 and 1854. Also, there is a new wiki (known as 'My Archives') whereby you can post additional information about a particular record or series of records.

In fact, the site actually contains at least three different catalogues. You can search them altogether (using the grandly names 'Global Search' engine) by using the cunningly hidden search button on the home page. In addition, you can order documents in advance. There are a number of on-line exhibitions, some on a military theme, and the Documents Online service where you can download scans of particular documents generally for a fee. For more about this, see Chapter 3, above.

www.nationalarchives.gov.uk

7. Britain's Small Wars

From the insect-ridden jungles of Malaya to the frozen hills of Korea, in the backstreets of Aden and Cyprus, from the African bush of Kenya to the rain soaked hills of the Falkland Islands, young National Servicemen and regular British soldiers have been defending British interests for six decades now. Their story is told at this extraordinary website. It is extraordinary, because as well as the usual (and informative) pages about the kit and the engagements fought, it features extremely honest and well written articles and comments by those who were there, both officers and other ranks, which is rather more than nostalgia for a lost youth one can find on lesser sites. Occasionally one gets a feeling that they may indeed be revealing things which perhaps still officially remains secret. This is particularly true for conflicts from the 1960s onwards. This is coupled with excellent design and easy navigation.

www.britains-smallwars.com

8. Naval Portmanteau Sites

For some reason, there are several excellent general websites on naval history. It is something that does not seem to be the case either for the Army or the Air Force, where most sites tend to concentrate on a particular topic. I have chosen five such sites as one top 10 website choice (it's my book after all!). They all do different things, although there some overlap and if you are studying the Royal Navy particularly in the twentieth century you will need to visit several of them.

The website of HMS *Surprise* http://home.wxs.nl/~pdavis/index.htm was originally a site about William Loney, a nineteenth-century naval surgeon, but has developed into a superb resource about the late eighteenth- and early nineteenth-century RN. You can even download software allowing you to 'navigate' HMS *Surprise* a Navy 'frigate' of the period, best known from the pages of Patrick O'Brian's novels – fascinating.

www.cronab.demon.co.uk offers a superb resource about the Royal Navy between the eighteenth and twentieth centuries, although it is pot luck whether you will find what you are looking for. Even if you don't, you are likely to be diverted into something more interesting. Unfortunately, it is hard to navigate around (you need to keep scrolling down the home page) and is very text heavy.

If you are researching the Navy in the twentieth century then Gordon Smith's

Naval History Net should definitely be visited at www.naval-history.net. There are pages about all aspects of the Royal Navy during, and between, the two world wars and the Falklands Campaign. It is at is best for the Second World War. There is also a sister site, www.worldwar1atsea.net, for the First World War period.

The next two are about aspects of the Second World War. http://uboat.net started life devoted to the U-boat campaign with details about all the German submarines, their captains and their fates. But it has broadened out into an excellent site about the Battle of the Atlantic and the Allied response to the U-boat threat. Meanwhile, www.fleetairarmarchive.net has a mass of material about the Fleet Air Arm, from detailed descriptions of the aircraft flown, histories of FAA Squadrons and rolls of honour for the men, as well as pages about the carriers they flew from.

9. Conscript Heroes

This book has dozens, may be hundreds, of websites devoted to the exploits and the memoirs of the famous, the infamous and the obscure. Many of the sites are excellent testimonies to the horrors and the humour of war. And it is only appropriate that at least one such site should be in my top ten choice, but which?

After consideration, I have chosen the website devoted to Peter Janes, who evaded capture by the Germans in 1940, and later made his way along the Pat O'Leary escape line to freedom in Spain. It is a fascinating story, well told by Janes's son, with a lot about escape and evasion in France in general. The site is well designed and well laid out with lots of illustrations, although, inevitably, there are few from the wartime period itself. You get a real feeling for the man and his experiences.

www.conscript-heroes.com

10. The Battle of Britain

For some reason there is a crop of excellent websites about the Battle of Britain, each of which is attractively designed and full of fascinating material. My favourite, partly because it is clearly is a labour of love, can be found at www.the-battle-of-britain.co.uk. It has lists of the squadrons and brief biographies of many of 'the Few' and technical descriptions of the planes. In addition, there is a day by day diary, and, chillingly, a speech made by Reichsminister Richard Darré reprinted here. If you want to know why the Battle had to be won, his speech is evidence enough!

www.the-battle-of-britain.co.uk

Appendix II

WEIRD AND ODD WEBSITES

Below I have chosen sites that cover unusual (or plain weird) subjects or which just amused me:

1. www.strange-mecha.com/index-e.htm is for the Strange Mechanism Museum of Japan, about experimental weapons and projects that never took off in the Japanese and German armies.

2. www.geocities.com/davidbofinger/ah.htm has pages of alternative histories. They are particularly interesting for the Second World War. There are links – via the webring to other sites on a similar theme.

3. http://ldb1.narod.ru/index2.html is an extremely slow loading site (in fractured English, German and Russian) about one Russian's experiences – Dmitry B Lomonosov – during the Second World War.

4. www.royalnavymemories.com/uckers is a generally entertaining and occasionally moving site about life in the post-war RN, but it wins its entry here by the superb page on 'Uckers', 'The Navy Game of Ludo', where visitors can learn 'to make the board and counters and to scrounge or thieve the materials to do a successful job'.

5. www.1879memorials.com/index.html is a somewhat eccentric site (if you are in doubt visit the page devoted to gravestones of fictional characters) tracing memorials of the men who fought during the Zulu War. You get a flavour of the hysteria of the chase and the strange things that happen to a group of obsessives.

6. http://myweb.tiscali.co.uk/janemarshallworld/
TweedalesWarPages%201–35.htm is the autobiography of Henry Tweedale of 232 Squadron. The navigation is very strange, and oddest of all, the memoir stops just as he captured by the Japanese in early 1942 without any warning – just as it was getting exciting!

7. www.kaiserlicherautomobilclub.de/english/inhalt.html is an unusual site devoted to the German Imperial Automobile Club, which had a military corps attached to it. You can listen to the Club song, 'Hurrah, Hurrah The Kaiser Is Coming'.

8. http://mysite.wanadoo-members.co.uk/wwihorse is an excellent site devoted to the role of horses in the First World War, with many interesting pages. Animals, and horsepower in general, were much used by both sides and their contribution has largely been forgotten. It is a pity that the site is no longer being updated.

9. www.scotcrash.homecall.co.uk is the wonderfully self-deprecating site of 'Two men and a dog [who] boldly go to seek out historic aircraft crash sites among the Hills, Munros and Mountains of Scotland', with some nice photographs.

10. Penguin Frog first produced plastic 1:72 models of military aircraft in 1936. The excellent and informative www.frogpenguin.com tells their story between then and 1947 and how models were used by the RAF during the war to train aircrew and others in identifying Allied and enemy aircraft.

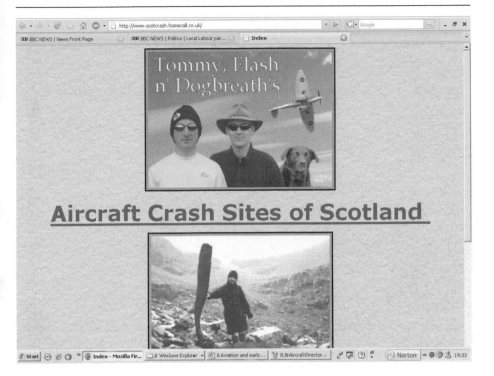